ONLY AUTHORIZED GUIDE IN AMERICA.

OFFICE OF THE PRESIDENT

St. Louis, March 19, 1904.

The Guide published by the Official Guide Company of St. Louis,
In accordance with the terms of its contract with this Company, is the
only Official Guide to the Louisiana Purchase Exposition the sale of
which is authorized in America by the Exposition Management.

David R Francis

President.

CASCADES AND FESTIVAL HALL.

OFFICIAL GUIDE

TO THE

LOUISIANA PURCHASE EXPOSITION

AT THE CITY OF ST LOUIS, STATE OF MISSOURI,
APRIL 30TH TO DECEMBER 1ST, 1904.

By Authority of the United States of America.

Containing an Historical Sketch of the Louisiana Purchase, and the
events leading up to the celebration thereof; a statement of
the Legislation relating to the Exposition, its form of
Organization and Government, and

A Full Account of all Features of the Exposition,

INCLUDING

Classification of Departments, Arrangement of Grounds,
Descriptions of the Palaces and Exhibits, the State, Territorial, Insular
and Foreign Buildings and Pavilions

Prepared by Chiefs of the Division of Exhibits,
Division of Exploitation, Division of Concessions and Division of Works,

WITH

INTRODUCTION BY PRESIDENT DAVID R FRANCIS

Profusely Illustrated with Original Half-Tones, Plan of Grounds and
Map of City

Compiled by M J LOWENSTEIN

Issued by Authority of the Louisiana Purchase Exposition.

ST. LOUIS:

THE OFFICIAL GUIDE CO.

ACKNOWLEDGMENTS.

The thanks of the publishers of this volume are due the following officials of the Louisiana Purchase Exposition for articles prepared by them and under their direction for use in the Official Guide: Hon David R Francis, President, Walter B Stevens, Secretary, Norris B. Gregg, Director of Concessions, F J V. Skiff, Director of Exhibits, Isaac S Taylor Director of Works, Edmund S Hoch, Assistant to Director of Exhibits; Halsey C Ives, Chief of Department of Art; John A Ockerson, Chief Department of Liberal Arts, M. C. Hulbert, Chief of Department of Manufactures and Varied Industries, Thos. M Moore, Chief of Department of Machinery, W E Goldsborough, Chief of Department of Electricity, Willard A. Smith, Chief of Department of Transportation; Frederic W Taylor, Chief of Departments of Agriculture and Horticulture, Tarleton H. Bean, Chief of Department of Forestry, Fish and Game, J A. Holmes, Chief of Department of Mines and Metallurgy, WJ. McGee, Chief of Department of Anthropology and Ethnology, Howard J Rogers, Chief of Department of Education and Social Economy; Jas. E. Sullivan, Chief of Department of Physical Culture, F. D. Coburn, ex-Chief of Department of Live Stock, Geo D. Markham, Chief of Bureau of Music; Mark Bennitt, Superintendent General Press Bureau, W. A. Kelso, Superintendent Local Press Bureau, R H Sexton, ex-Superintendent Publicity Bureau, Edward Hooker, Secretary Press and Publicity Committee, the late Col E C Culp, Secretary Committee on Ceremonies, John C Lebens, Local Press Bureau, Col. Sam Williams, Local Press Bureau, and others

INTRODUCTORY.

The publishers of the **Official Guide** present this volume to the visitors to the great Louisiana Purchase Exposition in the confident hope that it will prove an indispensable companion, serviceable in preliminary study, useful in directing a tour of the grounds and buildings, and valuable for after-reference because of its store of official data concerning the development of this most wonderful exhibition of human progress. Recourse has been had in the compilation of the book to official information, all the data in this respect having passed official scrutiny, both in preparation and final publication This sanction carries with it all the responsibility and weight of authority thereby implied.

All necessary material has been freely placed at the disposal of the publishers to the end that during the entire World's Fair period and for proper time beyond the **Official Guide** may be deemed essential to the ordinary visitor, the traveler, the historian and the publicist, in whose several lines and spheres of activity the Louisiana Purchase Exposition is, by its very magnitude and infinite variety, destined to play an important part

Not only has the **Official Guide** this, perhaps, general function, but its careful use and preservation will enable the purchaser to so arrange his St. Louis itinerary as to save him in full his most valuable asset; namely, time. Where whole civilizations, entire epochs, complete developments of peoples, their resources, manners and customs have been laid under contribution and epitomized, as in the case of the Louisiana Purchase Exposition, a publication equipped as is the **Official Guide** becomes an absolute necessity.

In contents, the **Official Guide** will be found to be complete and thorough, devoid of any superfluous matter and useless detail. It aims to fill the wants at the same time of the casual observer and the careful, painstaking student, and although, in a growing and inexhaustible project like this, the greatest World's Fair in the world's history, the need of future editions suggests itself, yet each edition is carefully revised and brought up-to-date The statistical information, roster of officials, list of events, illustrations and maps have all been prepared with the utmost care, with a view to making the **Official Guide** an inseparable adjunct to all Exposition patrons.

OFFICIAL GUIDE COMPANY.

THE EXPOSITION BUILDERS.

P. J. V. SKIFF, Exhibits.   ISAAC S. TAYLOR, Works.

WALTER B. STEVENS, Exploitation.   DAVID R. FRANCIS, President.   NORRIS B. GREGG, Concessions.

BENEFITS OF THE EXPOSITION.

Whether the United States, and especially St. Louis and the West, will derive from the Exposition material benefits of a money value equal to its cost, is a question sometimes asked by people who like to judge things by the "profit and loss" test.

The richest and most universal benefits to be expected from a great Exposition—its educational and moral benefits—can not be measured in terms of dollars and cents. They are legible only in general progress, in the radiance of home life, the halo of the national life, the intelligence and magnanimous efforts of the people.

In commemorating one of the most important events in the life of our Union, this Exposition has already rendered an inestimable public service by awakening a universal popular interest in the story of the Louisiana acquisition and its glorious results.

It has caused a gathering here of all the nations of the earth, each bringing comprehensive representations of the best productions of its arts and industries, its newest and noblest achievements, its latest discoveries, its triumphs of skill and science, its most approved solutions of social problems. . The far-reaching effect of such a vast display of man's best works on the intelligent and emulous minds of fifty or sixty millions of students, is beyond computation. Man's competitive instinct, the, spontaneous lever that arouses human activity and exalts human effort, directing it to higher standards of excellence, will surely work with a high potential current here. The impulse to excel the best and improve the latest improvements, operates in the United States with an aggressive force seldom exhibited in other countries. Its effects have been seen in the innumerable inventions and progressive steps following every great Exposition. This one will be an incomparable seminary of ideas and inspirations for people of all classes and avocations, and no one can doubt that such seed planted in our soil will bring forth a rich and abundant fruitage.

Fifty-three foreign governments are participating grandly in the Louisiana Purchase Exposition. Our Federal Government, and all the states of our great Union, are making here unparalleled displays of their boundless resources, their industrial progress and their ever-rising social status. The world has never before had so perfect a school for teaching the noble lessons of human worth and human brotherhood. From this school many millions of Americans will return to their homes, elated with a better appreciation of humanity at large and a far higher and prouder estimate of their own country and countrymen.

David R. Francis,
President.

LOUISIANA PURCHASE MONUMENT.

PLAN AND SCOPE OF THE EXPOSITION.

Estimates of Expenditure.—Around a nucleus of $15,000,000 contributed to the Exposition in equal parts by popular subscription, by the city of St. Louis and by the United States government, a total expenditure, estimated at $50,000,000, has grown. This amount is made up of the following items

City of St. Louis .	$ 5 000,000
Popular subscription	5,000,000
United States Government	11,000 000
States and Territories	7,000,000
Concessions .	6,000,000
Foreign Governments (buildings)	5,000,000
Foreign Governments (installation etc)	11,000,000
Total .	$50 000,000

Comparison of Expositions—This expenditure of money has produced the greatest and best Exposition in the history of the world. The ground area covered by it is 1240 acres. The Chicago Exposition covered 633 acres, that at Paris in 1900, 336, the Pan-American at Buffalo, 300 acres, the Centennial at Philadelphia, 236 acres; the Trans-Mississippi at Omaha, 150 acres. The Louisiana Purchase Exposition has under roof in the big exhibit palaces an area of 128 acres, the Columbian Exposition had 82 acres under roof, the Pan-American 15 acres and the Trans-Mississippi 9 acres The Palace of Agriculture, covering about 21 acres, at the Louisiana Purchase Exposition, contains more exhibit space than the entire Pan-American Exposition No former Exposition paid much attention to outdoor exhibits At St. Louis there are 100 acres of this class of exhibits, including the giant Bird Cage, the Mining Gulch, etc

Processes Rather than Products—The key-note of the Louisiana Purchase Exposition is life and motion. Moving exhibits predominate Processes are shown rather than products

Space Free.—No charge is made to exhibitors for space or power in any exhibit building

Day Sights and Night Scenes—The Exposition is made up of permanent features, like the buildings and grounds, and temporary or periodical features, like the concerts and the congresses The permanent features may be classified into day sights and night scenes The Exposition day begins for the sight-seer at 8 00 a. m , when the Exposition gates open. The exhibit palaces open one hour later The day ends at sunset, when all the exhibit palaces close with the exception of the Palace of Art, which is kept open at night at stated times The night scenes begin with the switching on of hundreds of thousands of electric lights The gates close at 11 30 o'clock

Outdoor and Indoor Views.—The day sights may be divided into outdoor and indoor The outdoor sights comprise the buildings and

MISSOURI BUILDING.

grounds Nearly 1,000 buildings compose the Exposition, counting all the small structures and the separate edifices of the Pike concessions. These buildings are of two kinds, service structures and show structures.

Service Structures.—The service structures are such as the power house, the garbage plant, the pump rooms, the hospital, the engine houses, the intramural stations, etc, which are all of surpassing interest to the specialist and are intended for the inspection of the visitor.

Show Buildings include the following· The exhibit structures comprising the giant palaces, each covering from four to twenty-one acres, of which there are fourteen, and the minor exhibit structures, like those in the Mining Gulch and the Model Street, the Indian School, the Anthropology building, the Physical Culture building, etc
The buildings erected by States and Territories, of which there are some forty-five, many of them reproductions of edifices for which the States are famous The forty acres of Philippine buildings and the three Alaskan buildings fall into this class
The Foreign Pavilions, of which there are about forty, each typical of the country that built it, and, in many cases, the reproduction of an historic building
Concession structures and the administration group of permanent college buildings

What the Grounds Offer.—In addition to the buildings, the outdoor sights comprise the sculptural decorations, water courses, gardens and other landscape effects. Almost every one of the foreign nations supplies a typical garden The Exposition itself shows a number of fine gardens as well as an expansive forest landscape
Decorative structures, including the Cascades and Lagoons, the Louisiana Purchase Monument, the approaches to the buildings located on hills, the music pavilions, the bridges, etc.

Exhibits, Displays and Amusements.—The indoor sights comprise the following· The exhibits of over 70,000 separate exhibitors, which are divided into fifteen departments and housed in the big exhibit palaces.
The historic exhibits and the fine furnishings in the State, Territorial and Foreign buildings These buildings are used as club houses and do not, except in case of Alaska, house the exhibits of the states and nations which erected them.
The concessions, which may be divided into historical, geographical, scientific, illusory, restaurant and selling concessions.
Night views of the Exposition are created principally by the lights. The buildings show a new architecture, the Cascades a new beauty.

Special Events.—The temporary, or periodical features of the Exposition include: Music in concerts and competitions by bands, organists, orchestras and choruses; conventions and congresses, athletic events, including the Olympic games, air-ship contests, military drills and encampments, social events, including the celebration of special days by nations, states, organizations and families.

ADMINISTRATION BUILDING.

HOW TO REACH THE FAIR GROUNDS.

Location of the Grounds.—The Fair Grounds are located about five miles from the west bank of the Mississippi river, or about four and one-half miles from the business section of the city.

Transportation to the Grounds.—(See map of the city.) The Fair Grounds are touched by transportation agencies from the city at eleven points. Two steam railroad terminals are close to the grounds. Nine electric street railway loop terminals, the lines of which serve all parts of the city for one fare, are located at the entrances. In addition, automobile and tally-ho coach lines, starting from the hotel section of the city, carry passengers to stations outside and inside the grounds. These transportation lines in detail are as follows:

Steam Railroads.—The Wabash Railroad has a fine terminal station at the main entrance to the Fair Grounds. Here thirty-two stub tracks, on which shuttle trains between the Fair Grounds and Union Station are operated, have been installed. Other steam railroads have made arrangements to use this terminal. The southern side of the grounds is reached by the Taylor City Belt Railroad, a corporation which serves the St Louis & San Francisco Railroad and the Missouri Pacific Railroad

Street Railways.—The street railways of St Louis are operated by two corporations, the Transit Company and the St. Louis & Suburban Railway Company. The former touches the Fair Grounds at six entrances, the latter at three entrances. Each system has its own transfers, but transfers are not interchangeable between the lines of the two companies. Passengers may reach the Fair Grounds for a single fare from any portion of the city. N. and S bound car lines cross E. and W bound lines (leading to the Fair) at more than a dozen different points. Transfers are issued by conductors of the Transit system at the request of passengers at the time the fare is paid and not afterwards. Conductors on the Suburban system offer transfers to all passengers when approaching transfer points.

St Louis street cars carry large lettered signs on the roof to indicate the line or street over which they travel. They carry other signs in the windows, front and back, and on the dashboards to indicate the route or destination or both.

One fare of five cents pays for a passage to the city limits from any point in the city. Children under 12 years are carried for half fare; under 5, free, the conductor issues a half-fare ticket as change for five cents when a child's fare is paid.

St. Louis Transit System Lines.—All electric cars of the St Louis Transit System going to the World's Fair Grounds carry blue enamel signs on the dashboard with the words, "Direct to the World's Fair Grounds."

Olive St. Line.—The most direct thoroughfare to the Exposition is Olive street. Three lines of the St Louis Transit System of electric cars traverse this street W. from Broadway to the Lindell entrance,

PLAZA OF ST. LOUIS.
Showing Louisiana Purchase Monument and Festival Hall.

through the best residence district These cars carry the word "Olive" on the roof

World's Fair cars traverse Olive street W. to Walton Av, thence S to McPherson Av, thence W. to Union Bl., thence S. to DeGiverville Av, stopping on the E loop near Lindell entrance. They return via the same route to Broadway

Olive St cars carrying the sign "Maryland," turn S at Boyle Av, thence W. on Maryland Av to Euclid Av, N on Euclid to McPherson Av., W on McPherson to Union Bl, thence S to DeGiverville Av and W to the E loop at Lindell entrance. They return via the same route to Broadway.

Olive St cars carrying the sign "Through," turn N from Olive St at Taylor Av, and thence W on Delmar Bl, transferring passengers at De Baliviere Av, to World's Fair cars (main entrance), W from De Baliviere Av to Hamilton Av, transferring to World's Fair cars (Pike and Administration Entrances), thence N to Easton Av. These cars if carrying a sign "Delmar Garden," proceed W on Delmar from De Baliviere Av to Delmar Garden and Delmar Race Track.

Delmar Av. Line—This line begins on Washington Av, passes W through the business district from Eads Bridge, and terminates at Lindell Entrance The cars turn N from Lucas Av on Grand Av to Finney Av, W to Taylor Av, S to Delmar Bl, W to De Baliviere Av, where they take the W loop at Lindell Entrance They return via practically the same route

Page Av Line—The Page Av. cars traverse Washington Av. from Eads Bridge to Grand Av, thence they turn N to Finney Av, W. to Taylor Av, N to Page Av., thence W to Hamilton Av, thence S. to The Pike and Administration Entrances; returning via the same route.

Easton Av Line—Cars with the large sign "Easton" on the roof, go W from Broadway on Franklin Av and Easton Av to Hamilton Av, thence S. on Hamilton Av and across a private right of way to The Pike Entrance

(The three loops at the N side of the Exposition grounds at Lindell, Pike and Administration Entrances are connected by an emergency line running E. and W. along the border of The Pike, and on occasion the cars may be interchanged from one of these roads to the other)

South Side Terminals—On the S border of the World's Fair Grounds there are two loops of the St. Louis Transit System, viz: at the State Buildings Entrance and Agriculture Entrance Three lines of cars take these loops. Laclede, Market and Taylor These alternate between the two loops according to conditions, but their designation is indicated by a white sign with black letters naming the entrance at which they stop

Laclede Av Line.—Cars bearing the word "Laclede" in large letters on the roof traverse Market St W from Fourth St, passing Union Station and proceeding via Laclede Av to Euclid Av., thence S to Chouteau Av., where they proceed by a private right of way to the loop at the State Buildings Entrance or the Agriculture Entrance; returning via the same route.

—17—

Taylor Av. Line.—Cars bearing the words "Taylor Av." in large letters on the roof, cross the city N. and S. on Euclid, Taylor and N. Newstead Avs. At Euclid and Chouteau Avs. they turn into a private right of way through Forest Park and proceed to the loops at the State Buildings Entrance or the Agriculture Entrance; returning via the same route.

Market St. Line.—Cars bearing the word "Market" in large letters on the roof, proceed from Fourth St. W. along Market St., passing Union Station, out Old Manchester Av. to Chouteau Av., and out Chouteau Av. W. to the loops at the State Buildings Entrance and Agriculture Entrance; returning via the same route.

From Union Station.—From Union Station, passengers may reach the Fair Grounds, either by taking the Laclede or Market St. lines, or by taking the Eighteenth St. line (going N.) and transferring to Olive St., Washington Av., or Franklin Av., (going W.)

Suburban System.—The St. Louis & Suburban (main line) electric cars, carrying sign on dashboard marked "World's Fair, Main Entrance," move from the business section W. on Locust St. to 13th St., N. on 13th and 14th Sts. to Wash St., continuing W. via Wash St., Franklin Av. and Morgan St., by a private right of way and Fairmount Av. to Union Bl., thence S. on **Union Boulevard** to Forest Park, pass under the Wabash Railroad tracks and West and follow the north edge of Forest Park to a loop opposite the Lindell Entrance S. of the Wabash Terminal Station.

Other Suburban main line cars, carrying dashboard sign marked "World's Fair, Skinker Entrance," over this same route pass W. from Union Bl. to **DeHodiamont**, thence W. and S. over a private right of way to Convention and Administration Entrances.

Transportation Facilities as estimated by experts connected with the Exposition Company, are as follows: The railroad and street car lines combined are able to handle 80,000 passengers to and from the Exposition grounds per hour. Street railroad schedules provide for an hourly traffic of 40,000 passengers.

CARTOUCHE ON FESTIVAL HALL.

OPENING DAY CEREMONIES, APRIL 30, 1904.

ENTRANCES TO THE GROUNDS.

The visitor should carefully study the excellent map of the grounds, to be found at the front of the **Official Guide**, in order to familiarize himself with the location of the various street car termini, entrances, buildings, etc.

Entrances—There are thirteen entrances to the grounds, serving not only the city of St Louis, which is located to the E of the grounds, but the county of St. Louis, which is located to the W. of the grounds The city limits pass through the Fair Grounds The E half of the Palace of Agriculture is in the city of St. Louis, the W half in the county of St Louis.

Main Entrance—The main entrance to the Exposition is at the N-E corner of the Fair Grounds. "The Main Picture" of the Exposition points to this entrance and the main central avenue leads toward it Two entrances are located at this point, one of which leads to The Pike or street of concessions, the other to the exhibit palaces in the main picture The great railroad terminal of the Wabash is located here and two Transit Company loops and one Suburban Company loop serve this entrance. In front of the gates of the Exposition a wide plaza designed for discharging passengers, is located.

Subsidiary Entrances—The other entrances to the Exposition, enumerating them in order of their location, are as follows· **The Pike** (Hamilton Av) Entrance leads into The Pike, or street of concessions, and is served by a Transit Company loop; **Administration Entrance**, located at Skinker Road (University Boulevard), is one of the principal subsidiary gateways. It supplies access directly to the pavilions of the foreign nations, the W. end of The Pike, or street of concessions, and the Administration group of permanent buildings It is served by both the St. Louis Transit Company and the St. Louis and Suburban Railway; **Convention Entrance**, served by the Suburban line, is designed for the admission to the Hall of Congresses without the payment of admission fees of delegates to Conventions and Congresses. If these delegates desire to enter the Fair Grounds from the Convention Hall, a fee is collected, **First County Entrance** is located close to the Physical Culture arena, where the Olympic games will be held It is designed principally as a vehicle entrance, **Second County Entrance** is located some distance S of the first, and is also a vehicle entrance, **Agriculture Entrance**, located at Skinker Road (University Boulevard), admits from the S and serves the live stock barns, the dairy barns, the camping grounds, the Palace of Horticulture and the Palace of Agriculture It is reached by the St Louis Transit Company; **South Railroad Entrance** is served by the Taylor City Belt Steam Railroad, supplying access for the St Louis & San Francisco and the Missouri Pacific railroads **Cheltenham Entrance** is located at Tamm avenue, and is served by the Transit Company; **State Buildings Entrance** is one of the principal of the subsidiary entrances; it is located at the S.-E corner of the grounds, is served by the Transit Company, and supplies access to the Plateau of States, on which the greater part of the State buildings are located; **Government Building Entrance** is reached only by vehicles or on foot, and serves directly the United States Government building; **Parade Entrance** is located some distance N. of the Government Building Entrance; it opens on Forest Park, and is used by the line of automobile tally-ho coaches and vehicles which enter the grounds. Parades enter the Exposition grounds by this gate.

DEFIANT INDIAN—By C. E. Dallin.
(West Court, Cascade Gardens.)

Liberal Arts.

VIEW ON LAGOON, LOOKING EAST.

U. S. Government.   Mines and Metallurgy.

Education.

GENERAL ASPECT OF THE GROUNDS.

Extent of the Grounds—The Exposition grounds are approximately in the shape of a rectangle, two miles from E to W and one mile from N to S. They are made up of four distinct parcels of ground, aggregating about 1,240 acres. The greater portion of the Fair is in the W. half of one of the largest public parks in the United States—Forest Park. The E half of this park has been kept intact. The Forest Park section of the Fair comprises 668 acres. It was the first portion of the site acquired, and on it are built eight of the big exhibit palaces. W of the Forest Park section is the Skinker tract acquired from private owners, the principal of whom was Thomas Skinker. It covers 422 acres. On it are located the Palaces of Agriculture, Horticulture, Forestry, Fish and Game, the Philippine reservation, the big Floral Clock, the plant Map of the United States, the United States life-saving exhibit, the Ethnology building, and the national pavilion of France. An area of 110 acres just N of the Skinker tract was leased from Washington University, an endowed educational institution of St Louis. On it are built the majority of the foreign pavilions and the Administration group of permanent buildings. E of the University tract and N of the Fair grounds is the Catlin tract, which contains sixty acres and is used entirely for concessions. The Pike runs the entire length of this tract, a distance of nearly a mile.

Hills on the Fair Grounds—The Louisiana Purchase Exposition is the first in which hills have helped the picturesque effect. "The Main Picture," made up of eight big exhibit palaces and a mile and a half of lagoon, is on a level area surrounded on two sides by hills that rise to a height of 65 feet. These hills are not continuous but jut out at four points. These jutting prominences are used with fine effect in the decorative scheme of the Exposition. The first of the prominences is crowned by the United States Government building. Two others, with the connecting ridge, form the Cascade effect. The remaining prominence is crowned by the national pavilions of Japan. The two central prominences, which are connected by a semi-circular ridge, lead to the lower level of the grounds by a finely sloping, hollowed declivity. This natural feature was used by the Exposition architects for what is pronounced by critics to be the greatest architectural, water and garden composition, ever executed by man, the Cascades and the Cascade Gardens. (For description of Cascades, see article on "Special Features of Interest." See also article on "Landscape and Gardens".) The declivity between the Cascades is occupied by lawns and gardens of exquisite design. The hill is reached from two of the avenues of the main picture by a long approach flanked by portrait statues of the great men who have helped in the development of the Louisiana Purchase.

Except the United States Government building, which has steel trusses, and the Palace of Art, which is a brick and stone building, all the big exhibit buildings of the Exposition are of wood and staff.

The color of the exhibit buildings is ivory white, with dashes of color on the roofs. This preserves the majesty of the white, while at the same time it lessens the strain on visitors' eyes.

The original Commission of Architects was composed of Widmann, Walsh & Boisselier, of St. Louis; Walker & Kimball, of Boston and Omaha; Van Brunt & Howe, of Kansas City; Eames & Young, of St. Louis; Carrere & Hastings, of New York; Barnett, Haynes & Barnett, of St. Louis; Cass Gilbert, of St. Paul and New York, and Isaac S. Taylor, of St. Louis, who was appointed Director of Works.

NAPOLEON—By Daniel C. French.
(Cascade Gardens.)

PALACE OF EDUCATION FROM GRAND BASIN.

TRIP AROUND THE GROUNDS.

Intramural Railroad—Every portion of the Fair Grounds, except the interior of The Pike and of the Main Picture, is served by a double track, overhead trolley, electric railroad, which runs partly on the surface and partly on an elevated structure, following the topography. It has a right-of-way seven miles long and fourteen miles of track Its two terminals, 600 feet apart, are located respectively E. and W. of the main avenue, so that they do not deface this fine central view Cars run at reasonable speed so that a passenger may make the trip between the terminals in about 10 minutes For a considerable portion of its route, the Intramural road skirts the enclosure of the Exposition For about two miles of its course, however, it runs directly through the heart of one of the most interesting portions of the Fair Grounds.

Trip on the Intramural.—As the visitor passes through the Lindell entrance to the Exposition, the first view that greets him is one of surpassing beauty The splendid palaces of Manufactures and Varied Industries, flanking the **Plaza of St. Louis**, lead the gaze across the Grand Basin to the Cascade Gardens and the magnificent dome of Festival Hall.

For an introduction to a stay, whether brief or protracted, at the Fair, nothing could be more satisfactory than a trip on the Intramural Railroad Station No 1, at the N.-E. corner of the Palace of Varied Industries is the point at which the journey begins For a third of a mile, the road skirts the N facade of the Varied Industries Palace on the left and pleasing structures of The Pike on the right At Station No 2, the first stop is made Here the **Plaza of St Anthony** affords a glimpse of the Directors' Club Pavilion that forms the W. terminus of the Colonnade of States. The view of the towers on Machinery Hall is soon cut off by the long facade of the Palace of Transportation, while The Pike, on the right, presents many novel buildings As the car passes Station No 3, the prospect opens and a host of beautiful pavilions appear Those on the S side of University Way are the buildings erected by Great Britain, China and Belgium, above which towers the stately dome of the Brazilian Pavilion Near at hand are the cottage of Bobby Burns, the Holland and Austrian Pavilions and the building that represents the Argentine Republic, while the view is crowned by the splendid Tudor Gothic group of Administration buildings, the permanent home of Washington University From Station No 4 the car passes the Aeronautic Course, the gymnasium and the Athletic Fields the latter being enclosed by the single tracks of the Intramural Railroad, the out-going cars stopping at Station No 5 and the incoming ones at Station No. 6

From Station No 5 to Station No 7 the most interesting part of the Ethnological exhibit area is traversed On the left is the Alaska Pavilion, surrounded by gayly colored totem poles, and on the right stands the Model Indian School There is a comprehensive view of the Palace of Forestry, Fish and Game, the French Pavilion grounds and the multitude of roofs and towers that adorn the Main Picture of the Fair Passing between Indian tepees, wigwams and other primitive dwellings on the right and the outside exhibits of the Horticulture department on the left, the car reaches the entrance to the Philippine Reservation at Station No 7 Here the Palace of Agriculture the Floral Clock, the Pavilions of Canada and Ceylon and the buildings in the vicinity of the Observation Wheel may be seen Approaching Station No 8, the Foreign

PALACE OF LIBERAL ARTS.

Pavilions of India and Guatemala appear in the foreground, with those of Brazil, Siam, Nicaragua and Cuba to the N.-E. Here the track runs between the U. S. Life Saving lake and the French Reservation, passing under the shadow of the Observation Wheel From Station No. 9 to Station No. 10 the track runs due S past the Rose Garden in front of the Palace of Agriculture, with the buildings of Japan, Jerusalem, Morocco, Illinois and California, showing at intervals South of the Palace of Horticulture, Station No. 10 is passed, and the track makes a wide curve around the wild animals of California, up past the Boer War Exhibit, through virgin forest to where, at Station 11, the Palace of Fine Arts may be seen From Station No 12 to Station No 13, the right side of the track presents nothing to the view but open country, while at the left are Grant's Log Cabin, the Oregon building and the structures at the end of the Mining Gulch. (For description, see "Special Features of Interest.") A wide sweep towards the S and E brings the car past the Inside Inn to Station No 14, thence past the State buildings of Iowa, Minnesota, Massachusetts, New York, Ohio, Wisconsin and Louisiana to the Missouri building and the U S Government Pavilion, near which is Station No. 15 Station No. 16 is at the end of the **Plaza of Orleans**, through which the Restaurant Pavilion forming the E terminus of the Colonnade of States may be seen The remainder of the road passes the Model City with the Palace of Manufactures in the background At Station No 17 the Louisiana Purchase monument and the Cascade Gardens are again presented

Fare.—The fare for the entire trip or between stations is ten cents Cars start from Stations 1 and 17, running in opposite directions, promptly at 8 a m, and leave the same stations, on their last trips, promptly at 11 30 p m

POINTS OF INTEREST ON THE INTRAMURAL RAILWAY.

Station No 1—Main Gate—Louisiana Purchase Monument Bank and Safe Deposit Cascades Express Offices Grand Basin Plaza of St Louis Automobile Stations Varied Industries Building (E End)

Station No 2—Pike Gate—Machinery Gardens, Band Stand Plaza of St Anthony. Gardens Varied Industries Building (W End). Transportation Building (F End) Machinery and Electricity Buildings

Station No 3—Skinker Gate—Administration Building and Gate Foreign Government Buildings Machinery and Transportation Buildings Pike (West Entrance)

Station No 4—Convention Gate—Aeronautic Concourse (Air Ship Exhibit) Anthropology, Inside Exhibit Hall of Congresses Convention Hall

Stations No 5 and 6—County Gate—Barracks and Parade Grounds Anthropology Outdoor Exhibit Athletic Field, Gymnasium Queen's Jubilee Gifts Olympic Games and Baseball

Special Stop—Indian School (On Signal Only)

Station No 7—Philippines—Arrowhead Lake Anthropology, Outdoor Exhibit Forestry, Fish and Game, Outdoor Missouri Wild Game U S Plant Map Tree Planting Indian Tepees Totem Poles

Station No 8—U S Life Savers—Agriculture Building Floral Clock Forestry, Fish and Game Building Foreign Government Buildings Ceylon Pavilion East India Pavilion

Station No 9—Agriculture Temple of Fraternity California Illinois, Japan

Station No 10—Agriculture Gate—Live Stock Arena Horticulture Georgia, Idaho Buildings Tennessee Maryland Buildings

Station No 11—Boer War

Station No 12—Art Palaces Festival Hall, Music Bureau Terrace of States Cascades

Station No 13—Cheltenham Gate—Plateau of States Germany

Station No 14—States Gate—Inside Inn State Buildings U S Bird and Fish

Station No 15—Government Gate—U S Fish Pond and Bird Cage Government Hill Guns and Coast Defences Liberal Arts Building Sunken Gardens Mines and Metallurgy Building U S Marine Corps Camp

Station No 16—Parade Gate- Emergency Hospital Model Street Liquid Air Exhibit Liberal Arts Plaza of Orleans, Manufactures U S Field Hospital Press Building

Station No 17 -Main Gate Plaza of St Louis Manufactures Building (W End)

SCULPTURE ON BUILDINGS AND GROUNDS.

The history and spirit of the Louisiana Territory are told by the
sculptor in more than one thousand figures that adorn the buildings
and grounds   They were executed by one hundred American sculptors at an expense of $500,000 00   The sculpture tells the story of the
great event commemorated by the Universal Exposition, the sway of
liberty from the Atlantic to the Pacific, through the acquisition of
the Louisiana Territory • Historic figures and groups emphasize its
national significance, allegorical statuary expresses those purely joy-
ous and festive fancies arising out of such a commemoration   The
sculpture reflects the larger and grander phases in the adventurous
lives of those explorers and pioneers who won the wilderness from
its brute and barbarian inhabitants as well as those achievements of
later civilization, wrought by the genius of American intellect

The fancy of the sculptor has been given the wildest latitude, and
allegory reaches the boldest flights of the imagination.   Beginning
with the decoration of Festival Hall the sculptural masses portray
the liveliest and most extravagant symbols of pleasure and pure
abandon

The climax of the designer's ideal, the hill that is crowned by
Festival Hall, is replete with sculptured groups of power and beauty
The Victory that surmounts the splendid dome, the first Victory to
take the form of a man, was modeled by a woman, Miss E B Longman

H A MacNeil's massive fountain, 'The Triumph of Liberty''
forms an allegorical veil before the entrance to the Hall of Festivals
"Liberty," "Justice" and Truth" dominate, from a serene height,
other groups, symbolical of the human qualities which spring from
and are fostered by liberty   From this heroic mass issue the waters
of the Main Cascade   On pedestals along the successive water-leaps
are fine attendant figures, expressing the growth and progress of
liberty and civilization.

The East and West Cascades seem to be fed by fountains that
are symbolic of the Atlantic and Pacific Oceans   The East Cascade is
dominated by "The Spirit of the Pacific," showing the airy figure of
a graceful girl, floating in space, attended by an albatross, the winged
genius of that calm water. "The Spirit of the Atlantic," surmounting
the West Cascade, embodies the splendor of full womanhood.

The Colonnade of States, a peristyle swinging around the W of
the gardens and connecting Festival Hall with two elaborately finished kiosks, is treated ornately with statuary of heroic mould.   At
regular intervals along the terrace, in front of the Colonnade, are
seated female figures, emblematic of the fourteen states developed

PALACE OF MANUFACTURES.

from the Louisiana Purchase Territory The Colonnade, itself, is embellished with groups crowning the summits of its terminals

A wealth of statuary in permanent form enriches the main building of the Fine Arts group

History takes the place of Allegory along the approaches to the Cascade Gardens, by way of successive flights of broad pink stairways leading from the levels of the Plaza of St Anthony and the Plaza of Orleans to the summits of the terminals on the Terrace of States

Along the lagoon in the Plaza of St Louis, are four groups, full of the spirit of the frontier "A Peril of the Plains," the last of the four, is a wonderfully realistic picture of a trapper and his horse caught in a winter's storm on the plains

Back of these is formed one of the principal decorative features of the Exposition This is the Louisiana Monument, 100 feet high that rises from the center of the Plaza of St. Louis The monument is the conception of E L Masqueray, designer-in-chief of the Exposition. Four groups of statuary form part of the ensemble of the monument, erected to commemorate the American genius which subdued the forces of nature and savagery in the new world inland empire Karl Bitter, chief of sculpture, furnished the statue of "Peace," crowning the shaft, as well as all the groups assembled at its base

At the extreme N end of the Plaza of St. Louis in direct line with the Hall of Festivals and the Louisiana Monument, is another of the principal decorative features, entitled "The Apotheosis of St. Louis" Charles H Niehaus is the sculptor of this fine historical theme The group symbolizes the cordial welcome extended by the City of St Louis to her guests from every part of the world Towering fifty feet into the air is a massive equestrian statue of the crusader St. Louis, for whom the Exposition city is named At the base of the pedestal, on which the king and his charger are mounted, is a seated female figure, symbolic of the matron "St Louis," who bespeaks the far-famed hospitality of the World's Fair city In her generously outstretched hands she holds an endless scroll recording her civil glories Besides her are the youthful figures of 'Inspiration" and "Genius" This emblematic figure has been selected to adorn the cover of the Official Guide

Equestrian statues of early Spanish explorers embellish the E and W. sides of the Plaza, between the Louisiana Purchase Monument and the "Apotheosis" Two other notable equestrians have conspicuous places 'A Sioux Chief Defying Advancing Civilization," by Cyrus E Dallin, occupies the first terrace at the head of the Plaza of St. Anthony, and its companion piece, "A Cherokee Chief" by J E Fraser, similarly located at the head of the 'Plaza of Orleans"

PALACE OF VARIED INDUSTRIES FROM GRAND BASIN.

SCULPTURE ON THE BUILDINGS

The sculpture on the Palaces is as follows:

PALACE OF MANUFACTURES

Quadriga over main entrances, by Charles Lopez and F. G. R. Roth
"Progress of Manufactures," groups on pylons flanking main entrance, by Isidore Konti
"Victory," main entrance, by Michael Tonetti
"Energy" and "Power," groups flanking E and W entrances, by L. O. Lawrie
Casque with flags, and female figures with eagle-crowned shields, on roof line, by L. Amateis
"Fountain of Neptune" and "Fountain of Venus," flanking N and S entrances and corner pavilions, by Philip Martiny
Spandrels over all doors, by G. T. Brewster
Seated figures in main entrance, by Zolnay, Packer and Heber
Greek Sphinx on block pedestals in front of colonnade, marking smaller entrances, Anonymous

PALACE OF TRANSPORTATION.

Group with shield, in curving entablature over all main entrances, by Paul Wiehle
"Transportation by Rail" and "Transportation by Boat" seated figures at base of corner towers, by George J. Zolnay
"Spirit of Transportation" figure for crown pylons, by F. F. Horter
Seated figures flanking main entrances, by F. H. Packer and Carl Heber
Figure at base of towers, by William Sievers

PALACE OF MINES AND METALLURGY

"Coal," "Iron," "Gold," "Copper" above frieze line, on screen wall, four figures by Charles Mulligan
Architectural figures between columns, by F. W. Ruckstuhl
"Torch-bearer" and attendant figures, and frieze at base of obelisks, by Rudolph Schwarz
Frieze on screen wall between columns, by Theodore Baur

PALACE OF VARIED INDUSTRIES

Tympanum group, E pediment, by Clement T. Barnhorn
Tympanum group, S pediment, by Douglas Tilden
Torch-bearer, repeated ten times above entablature of swinging colonnade, by Bruno L. Zimm
Lions, surmounting pylons, S entrance, by F. W. Ruckstuhl
"Industry of Man" and "Industry of Woman," seated figures between columns E facade, by Antonin C. Skodik
Symbolic groups, E and W entrances by John Flanagan
Figures for N entrance and four figures, W cornice, by F. W. Ruckstuhl
Spandrels, bas-relief W. entrance, by Peter Rossak
Spandrels, bas-relief corner towers, by William W. Manatt

PALACE OF EDUCATION

All statuary by Robert Bringhurst
Quadriga over main entrances
"Goldenrod," architectural figure, repeated six times over entrance colonnades
"Thread of Fate," flanking quadriga
"Flight of Time," flanking quadriga
"Music" group on block pedestal right of each main entrance
"Manual Training," group on block pedestal left of each main entrance
"Archaeology" and "Music," spandrels in the round, over large doors
"Geography" and "History," spandrels in the round, over small doors

PALACE OF MACHINERY.

"Labor and Care" tympanum group, repeated over six entrances, by Fernando Miranda
"Shield Holders," repeated eight times, E and N entrances, above cornice by A. A. Weinmann
"Atlas with Globe," colossal group, N facade, by R. H. Perry
Spandrels for W facade, by Anton Schaif
Spandrels, bas-relief, E and N facades, by Melva Beatrice Wilson
Group over N pavilion, by Max Mauch

PALACE OF ELECTRICITY.

"Light Overcoming Darkness," group crowning pyramidal corner towers, and "Wonders of the Lightning" and "Wonders of the Aurora" on corner towers, by Bela Pratt
"Light," "Heat," "Speed," "Power," four seated figures above pairs of projected columns on E facade, by August Lukemann
"Electricity," group over main entrance, by Charles Grafly

PALACE OF ELECTRICITY FROM GRAND BASIN.

UNITED STATES GOVERNMENT BUILDING.

All statuary by James E. Fraser

Tympanum in alto rclief Romanesque ornament for pediment over main entrance
"Liberty Triumphant" groups flanking pediment
"Liberty Victorious," quadriga crowning central dome
"Liberty," inside building, replica of Liberty on dome of Capitol at Washington

FESTIVAL HALL

"Victory," crowning dome, gilded, by Evelyn B. Longman
"Music," by August Lukeman and "Dance," by M. Tonetti flanking main entrance
"Apollo and Muses," by Philip Martiny
Cartouche, with two figures above main entrance, by John Pike

PALACE OF LIBERAL ARTS.

Quadriga, with two attendant groups, over main entrance, by Charles Lopez and
    F. G. R. Roth
"Music" and "Learning," groups flanking main entrance, by George E. Bissell
"Apotheosis of Liberal Arts," groups on end pylons, by H. Linder
"Ceramics" and "Invention" figures on four corners of end pylons, by D. P. Pedersen
"Pottery Decoration," figure over door in end pavilion, by C. Y. Harvey
Cupids with shields, above entablature, by Philip Martiny
Reclining figures, over broken pediment of central door, by Edith B. Stevens

MAIN CASCADE.

All sculpture by H. A. MacNeil
"Fountain of Liberty" chateau d'eau at head of cascade
"Physical Strength" balanced by
"Physical Liberty," on first cascade leap
"Cupid with Dolphin" on successive leap
"Pegasus and Sea Nymphs" on last leap

SIDE CASCADES

All sculpture by Isidore Konti
"Atlantic Ocean" fountain at head of W. cascade
"Pacific Ocean," at head of E. cascade
"Progress of Navigation" balanced by
"Progress of Commerce" on first leaps
"Grace and Strength"
"Cupid Holding Fish"
"Girl with Petrel"
"Sea Sport"
"Fisheries," on successive leaps

TERRACE OF STATES

Each figure in its own shrine, the Colonnade being formed of seven hemi-cycles on each side of Festival Hall
"Missouri," by Sterling A. Calder "Arkansas" by Albert Jaegers, "Louisiana," by Rudolph Schwartz "Iowa," by Carl E. Tefft "Nebraska" by E. H. Parker "Kansas," by Adolph A. Weinmann "Oklahoma" by I. S. Conway "Indian Territory," by C. A. Heber "Colorado," by August Zeller, Jr "Minnesota" by Gustav Gerlach, "North Dakota," by Bruno P. Zum "South Dakota," by L. O. Lawrie, "Montana" by Antonin C. Skodik, "Wyoming" by C. F. Hamann
Bear for Lampadcire of Colonnade, by F. G. R. Roth
"Strength," group surmounting W. terminal pylon, by Vincenzo Alfano
Groups at E. end of Colonnade by Alexander Ruel

PALACE OF FINE ARTS.

"Inspiration" bronze for pinnacle of pediment, by Andrew O'Connor
"Sculpture," beside entrance, by Daniel C. French
"Painting," beside entrance, by Louis St. Gaudens
"Truth," E. niche of central pavilion by Charles Grafly
"Nature," W. niche, by Philip Martiny
"Classic Art," limestone, above porch, by F. E. Elwell
"Renaissance Art" limestone, by Carl E. Tefft
"Oriental Art" limestone, by Henry Linder
"Egyptian Art," limestone by Albert Jaegers
"Gothic Art," limestone, by Johann Gelert
"Modern Art" limestone, by C. P. Hamann
Eleven medallions, limestone, by G. T. Brewster
Eleven medallions, limestone, by O. Piccirilli
Two griffins, copper, by Phimister A. Proctor
Two centaurs, at ends of pediment
Thirty antique figures for temporary wings

Twenti-six antique figures for permanent wings
Panels over porch, by H A McNeil

PORTRAIT STATUES.

"Horace Mann," W entrance to Palace of Education, by H K Bush Brown
"Pestalozzi," N entrance to Palace of Education, by A Jaegers
' Joseph Henry," E entrance to Palace of Electricity, by J Flanagan
'Benjamin Franklin," N entrance to Palace of Electricity, by John Boyle
"Charles Goodyear," S entrance to Palace of Manufactures, by Michael Tonetti
'Jehan Gobelin ' E entrance to Palace of Varied Industries, by Max Mauch
Right approach to Cascades
    "Lienville" and ' M Lewis," by Charles Lopez
    ' Daniel Boone ' by Enid Yandall
    "G R Clark," by Elsie Ward
    ' W Clark " by F. W Ruckstuhl
    ' Sieur La Salle," by L Gudebrod
    "Pere Marquette," by C E Dallin
    "Thomas Jefferson," by Charles Grafly
    ' Napoleon," by Daniel C French.
Left approach to Cascades
    ' Panfilo Narvaez," by H Adams
    "James Madison," by Janet Scudder
    ' Robert Livingston," by A Lukemann
    ' James Monroe," by Tuba Bracken
    ' Marbois by H Hering
    "Andrew Jackson " by L Potter
    "Philippe Renault " by A S Calder
    "Anthony Wayne ' by W C Noble
    'Pierre Laclede," by J Hartley

STATUARY ON THE GROUNDS

MAIN AVENUE
' The Mountain' and 'The Plain," by Lorado Taft
' Pastoral " by C A Heber
Indian Fountain group, by A A Weinmann

WEST COURT.
' Sioux Chief, ' equestrian, by C E Dallin

EAST COURT
"Cherokee Chief ' equestrian, by J E Fraser
' Cheyenne Chief " by F Remington

PLAZA OF ST LOUIS
"Apotheosis of St Louis by C H Niehaus
"De Soto," equestrian, by E C Potter
' Louis Joliet," by A P Proctor

LOUISIANA PURCHASE MONUMENT
All figures by Carl Bitter
"Peace," on globe surmounting shaft.
' Signing of the Treaty "
'Spirit of the Missouri River" and
"Spirit of the Mississippi River," at base

MAIN LAUNCH LANDING
Four groups by Solon Borglum
' Buffalo Dance "
"A Step to Civilization '
"Cowboy at Rest "
"Peril of the Plains "

EAST LAUNCH LANDING.
' Combat of Grizzly Bears" and "Combat of Sea Lions," by F G R Roth

WEST LAUNCH LANDING.
"Combat Between Bull and Cougar" and ' Cougar Attacking Dying Cow," by E C Potter

ENTRANCE TO PIKE.
'Shooting up the Town," by F Remington

PALACE OF MACHINERY.

LANDSCAPE AND GARDENS.

Surrounded on three sides with primeval forests, and embracing hill and valley plateau and lowlands, precipitous ravine and gently undulating slope, the ground on which the Louisiana Purchase was built, afforded the architects opportunity for beautiful effects such as were denied the builders of former Expositions. The World's Fair designers seized every natural advantage and turned it to profit.

The result is a city of ivory palaces of matchless grandeur and unequaled beauty of architecture created apparently, in the heart of a forest.

We may turn whichever way we will and vistas of glorious beauty appear before us. We may traverse the thirty-five miles of the Exposition roadway, through the wide avenues between stately palaces or over the narrower and densely-shaded roads of the wooded sections, and see a constantly varying and ever beautiful landscape.

Gardeners of all the nations of the world have united in producing this landscape masterpiece of all ages. Before one has a chance to tire of the beauties of one prospect one is lost in admiration of another equally entrancing.

Cascade Gardens.—The most elaborate of the formal gardening is upon the slope of what is popularly known as the Cascade Gardens, in the southern part of the central picture, south of the Grand Basin, which lies between the Education and Electricity buildings. The feature is half a mile in length, extending in a long southern sweep around the end of the Basin and the communicating lagoons. The slope is 300 feet wide with a rise of 60 feet.

Between and beyond the Cascades are the great lawns, with their rich embroideries of flowers. Cement walks and flights of easy steps are provided throughout the vast gardens, and a liberal use of sculpture completes the decorative detail.

Another garden of special prominence is situated in front of the United States Government building, in full view from the main transverse avenue. The same advantage attaches to the **sunken garden** between the Palace of Liberal Arts and the Mines and Metallurgy building. (See article on "Special Features of Interest.")

In the landscape work, throughout the central picture large trees are an essential part of the decoration.

Agriculture Hill gave the landscape gardener a rare chance. On the east side of the great Palace of Agriculture is the largest **rose garden** in the world. (For description, see article on Special Features of Interest.) Adjoining the rose garden are special exhibits of flowering plants such as geraniums, peonies, cannas, dahlias, caladiums, tube roses, etc.

South of the rose gardens are the aquatics. Here, in a series of graceful lakes, connected with winding lagoons, and spanned by rustic bridges, are seen growing all the water plants. The lotus of the Nile, the water hyacinth brightly-colored water poppies, graceful umbrella palms, and scores of other plants come in for their share of admiration. Here the Victoria Regia, transplanted from her home in the Amazon, has been carefully nurtured until her broad leaves are six feet across and possess such strength that a man's weight is borne with ease.

Between the Palaces of Agriculture and Horticulture are the Gardens of the Desert—plants that thrive in arid places, in sand, amid rocks and in spots that one would think nothing of life could survive. These plants, that derive their sustenance from the air and care naught for the moisture of the earth, produce blossoms and foliage of rare beauty.

The striking feature of the great terrace on the north side of Agriculture Hill is the great floral clock. (See article on "Special Features of Interest.")

In the Wild Garden, two acres in extent, on the west slope of Agriculture Hill, we may seek the shade of a giant oak, and revel among the buttercups and daisies. We may turn and listen to the babble of the brook as it runs through the garden, over its rocky bed and beneath the exposed roots of gnarled oaks and pours over miniature falls on its way to a graceful lake filled with plants.

English Garden—A replica of the Orangery of the Kensington Palace, is surrounded by an English country seat garden of 200 years ago. Hedges are a prominent feature, and the borders give the gardens a distinctly English appearance. The hollyhock, pre-eminent two centuries ago, is one of the flowers prominent in this garden of old England. There are old-fashioned roses, the juniper and yew, and other shrubs, some so pruned that they take on the forms of lions and peacocks and other birds and animals. Perhaps the most English of any of the features of this old garden is the pleached alley extending along the east side of the Orangery tract. Rows of poplars, planted in parallel, form the side walks. Their branches meet and cross each other overhead forming almost a roof of shade, through which flickers just enough sunshine to afford the proper degree of light.

French Garden—The treatment of the French Gardens of Versailles, about the Grand Trianon, is very elaborate. The French Government reservation covers fifteen acres. The center driveway is flanked on both sides by raised terraces of sward, and shaded by parallel rows of parked Carolina poplars. The slopes along the driveways and tableland of the terraces are done in the finest example of French floral embroidery. Statuary intersperses the arcade of trees. To the south of the drive, across the terrace gardens, the ground falls away to lower levels in a series of terraces, solidly banked with French horticulture. Outspread on a great level, running away from the foot of the terraces, is the gem of the French display, a beautifully fashioned landscaping set in bas-relief. To the west and flanking the south side of the Trianon, the gardeners have introduced a profusion

PALACE OF TRANSPORTATION

of exotic beauty which is permitted to follow the vagaries of Nature. A continuance of this treatment is carried around the west and north fronts of the pavilion. Tiny lakes give the same section of the garden a touch of nature unadorned. The court of the Trianon itself, formed by the central building and its L-shaped wings, has a pavement of pink gravel, cooled by a splashing fountain. (See article on "France.")

Chinese Garden.—The use of Prince Pu Lun's country seat for the Chinese National Pavilion furnishes a royal excuse for pilfering from the **Imperial Gardens at Pekin.** The garden effect was designed by Madame Wong Kai Kah, wife of the Imperial Chinese Vice-Commissioner of the Exposition. An open court in the center of the Chinese Pavilion is a feature.

German Garden.—Surrounding Germany's magnificent building, on the summit of a high hill overlooking the Cascades, are copies of the famous **Charlottenburg Gardens.** Many of the plants in the reproductions at the World's Fair were grown in Germany. The spacious driveways leading to the entrances of the palace are beautified by beds of fragrant blossoms and clumps of picturesque shrubbery, trained in the ideal German style.

Japanese Garden.—Japanese gardeners took advantage of their commanding site on the hill forming the western boundary of the Cascade territory to create some bewilderingly beautiful gardens. They have reproduced some of the famous sections of the gardens that surround **the Mikado's palace.** Only partially concealed by the dwarf shrubs and gorgeous flowers are dainty pagodas and quaint fountains.

Other Gardens.—Sweden, Cuba, Mexico and many other foreign nations, besides nearly every State and Territory in the Union, contribute their quota to the production of a beauty spot that extends over an area of two square miles and has never been equaled elsewhere in the world.

PALACE OF FINE ARTS.

SPECIAL FEATURES OF INTEREST.

A number of special features which belong to the several exhibit departments are unusually attractive, and stand out in importance as objects worthy of independent description

Artistic Wood Carving—There are some magnificent specimens of wood carving in the foreign pavilions In France's building, S.-W. corner, some elaborate and beautiful work is displayed   Other fine examples of carved interior wood work are the banqueting hall of the British Pavilion, which shows Corinthian columns and ornamental panels carved in poplar and stained to imitate walnut, and the Eichenholzgalerie on the second floor of the German Pavilion, which is a reproduction of the same chamber in the Charlottenburger Schloss, and which is entirely in oak, with details picked out in gilt   Forty thousand dollars was expended by the Chinese government in wood carvings for its National Pavilion

The Cascades—The striking feature of the Exposition and about which the whole picture is arranged, is the magnificent architectural and decorative composition known as the Cascades   They with the Art Palace, the Terrace of States, the Festival Hall, and the two pavilions, form the point of the fan in which the exhibit palaces are grouped

The Cascades are three in number, and far surpass in size and beauty any work of like character ever seen in the history of the world   By far the largest of the three is the central Cascade   This has its beginning in an artistic hood, or veil, just in front of Festival Hall, which stands out from the center of the Terrace of States.   The water gushes forth from this fount 24 feet above the level of the terrace, spreads out into a stream 45 feet wide and 11 inches deep, and leaps from weir to weir, down the long slope of ledges or steps spreading to a width of 150 feet as it takes its final plunge into the Grand Basin

This **Grand Basin** is semi circular in shape and 600 feet in diameter   No handsomer artificial basin can be found anywhere in the world

The side Cascades have their sources in fountains in the center of large basins in front of each of the pavilions which stand at either end of the Terrace of States   Four magnificent jets d'eau, or artificial geysers, arise from the Grand Basin at the foot of the side Cascades   On a quiet day these fountains throw streams which attain a height of 75 feet   The three Cascades issue from appropriate sculptures at the top of the hill, or terrace and by a series of descents down steps, plunge into the basin below   As all the buildings and avenues of the Exposition radiate from this feature, the glint and sparkle of the down-pouring waters are visible across a vast expanse from all the thoroughfares of the main picture   Along the edges of the Cascades, powerful vertical and horizontal jets of water issue from artistic sculptures and fall into the Cascade basin   These jets serve both to agitate the water, adding to its picturesqueness and to reinforce the supply as it spreads over the widening ledges   Over these three Cascades the immense volume of 90,000 gallons of water descend every minute   The machinery for pumping this vast quantity of water is located beneath the side Cascades, and has a capacity sufficient to elevate the water to a height of approximately 90 feet   It

PALACE OF MINES AND METALLURGY.

is probably the largest pumping outfit ever installed. Rough construction work on the Cascades, including grading, framing of basins lining of basins, and granitoid steps with copings, cost $120,000 in addition to the balustrades, staircases, etc, which cost about $100 000.

At night the Cascades and their surroundings are the focus of a splendid electrical illumination, and the entire picture is one of surpassing loveliness by day and by night

Devil in Sulphur.—In the Louisiana exhibit in the Palace of Mines, are shown a statue of the Devil in sulphur and **Lot's wife** in rock salt

Floral Clock—In addition to an extensive display of clocks in the Varied Industries Palace proper, and the Electric Clock in the court of the Palace of Electricity, one of the most novel features of the Exposition is the floral clock on Agriculture Hill, for which the Department of Manufactures furnishes the mechanism   This consists of a dial 100 feet in diameter, the numerals on which are approximately 15 feet high, and made entirely of flowers   At the top of the dial is a small house built to contain the mechanism, and adjoining it are two others containing a 5,000-pound bell, whose tones can be heard at a great distance and a mammoth hour-glass exposed to view.   This bell strikes the hour and half hour, and upon the first stroke of each hour the immense hour-glass turns so that the sand runs back   At the same time the doors of the house swing open, exposing the mechanism which controls the striking and operates the dial, and closing immediately upon the last stroke of the bell At night the clock is brilliantly illuminated, and 1,000 lamps are required for this purpose

Grand Pipe Organ, in Festival Hall, entered as an exhibit through the Liberal Arts Department, is the largest organ in the world, constructed by a Los Angeles, Cal, company   It covers a space 33 feet wide, 62 feet long, and is 40 feet high It has fine manuals, 140 speaking stops, 239 movements and 10 059 pipes, and is of itself one of the marvels of the Exposition   This organ required a train of 14 cars for its transportation   All modern improvements in organ building are met with this instrument   It will be played upon in daily recitals by celebrated organists, among them M Alexander Guilmant, of Paris   (See article on "Music at the Exposition")

Historic Fire Arms—In the center of the western part of the Palace of Forestry, Fish and Game is the most remarkable collection of fire-arms in the world The exhibit shows the development of the fire-arm from its crudest state It begins with the bow gun, from which arrows and heavy stones were fired, the power being simply the elasticity of the wood, as in the Indian bow It passes through the stages of the wide-mouthed blunderbus, the flintlock and the muzzle-loader to the modern breech-loading army rifles and fowling pieces The latest type in the collection is a weapon obtained from the United States Government showing the arm now being manufactured for the use of the United States troops A number of cannon are also in the collection The collection is valued at $50 000, the most cherished single piece being a Cookson gun made over 400 years ago in London, and which is inlaid with silver and gems.

Interesting Exhibits—A reproduction of the Southwest Pass lighthouse and an equatorial telescope, weighing 4,000 pounds, are to be found in the Palace of Liberal Arts —Methods of manufacturing small arms for the American soldiers are shown in the United States Government building —The historic stage coach used by Emperor Maxi-

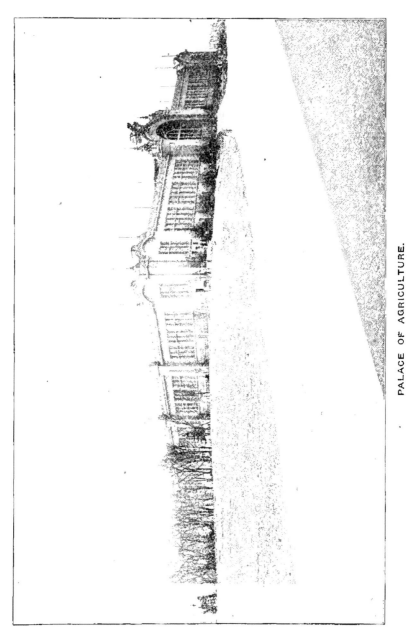

PALACE OF AGRICULTURE.

milian during his reign over Mexico is shown among the exhibits of that country in the Palace of Transportation. It is gorgeously ornamented with pearls, gold and silver The coach, which is considered Mexico's greatest heirloom, came direct from the National Museum at Mexico City—Hank Monk stage coach; this famous old coach is one of Colorado's exhibits in the Palace of Transportation This is the coach in which Horace Greeley and other famous men rode Mark Twain tells a story of this old conveyance in one of his books The coach was attacked 56 times by stage robbers, and 30 persons were killed in these encounters—The Idaho silver nugget, in Palace of Mines and Metallurgy, weighs ten tons—There is a working display of the big guns of the United States outside the Government building —Chief Geronimo and Chief Joseph are among the noted Indians on exhibition at the Fair—Carolina exhibits, in Palace of Forestry, a tree 800 years old

Map in Wood.—In the Varied Industries building is a drawing room table made of over 40 different kinds of wood, so inlaid as to form a perfect map of the United States A United States flag and the official flag of the Exposition, with the fleur-de-lis surrounded by stars, shown in opposite corners of the table, are the only bits of color in it

Plant Map of the U. S—This gigantic map of the United States in growing plants is located just west of the Palace of Forestry Fish and Game, and was installed by Government Bureau of Plant Industry of the Department of Agriculture The map occupies five acres, and each State is represented by native plants and grasses, a total of 819 distinct species of plant life Gravel walks mark the state and coast lines, and each State is appropriately labeled The entire five acres have been underlaid with wooden drains to carry off the surface waters The waste places around the margins of the map, resulting from the irregular coast line of the United States, are used for plant exhibits of various kinds Classes of public school children work on the map daily It cost $10 000

Rose Garden.—Located on the east side of the Palace of Agriculture, is the largest rose garden in the world It covers nearly ten acres, and within its borders are growing thousands of rose bushes clothed in the gorgeous raiment of more than a million blossoms

Solar Engine—A priest from Lisbon, Portugal, who is Professor of Science in a college in Parto and Coimbra, M A G, Himalaya, proposes to establish, under the auspices of the Portuguese Commission, west of the Palace of Forestry, Fish and Game, a mammoth solar engine, weighing 30 tons, and whose dimensions are 100 feet by 60 feet By a system of giant converging lenses the rays of the sun can be focused to a point It is claimed that the machine will melt anything

Statue of Vulcan—A colossal statue of Vulcan occupies a conspicuous place in the center of the Palace of Mines and Metallurgy The statue is made of iron and is a part of the exhibit of mines and metallurgy contributed by the iron manufacturers of the city of Birmingham, Alabama The statue is 56 feet high and weighs 100,000 pounds A horse and buggy may be driven between its feet. The dimensions of its various parts are Length of face, 7 feet 6 inches; foot, 6 feet; arm, 10 feet, breadth of back 10 feet, measurement of chest, 22 feet 9 inches, waist, 18 feet 3 inches, neck, 11 feet 6 inches Weight of anvil block, 6,000 pounds, weight of spear head, 350 pounds,

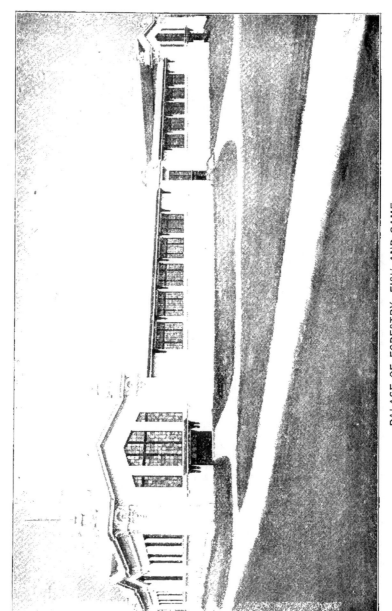

PALACE OF FORESTRY. FISH AND GAME.

weight of hammer, 300 pounds. Cost, $20,000. The plaster cast for the Vulcan was made at Passaic, N. J. Three 60-foot cars were required to transport the cast to Birmingham, where it was moulded and cast into iron. After the Exposition period the Vulcan will be returned to adorn a public park at Birmingham.

THE MODEL STREET.

The Model Street is an exhibit of the Municipal Improvement Section of the Department of Social Economy, the plan being to create higher standards of street equipment and city arrangement by practical suggestions from experts and by comparison of

MUSIC
(Palace of Liberal Arts.)

UNITED STATES GOVERNMENT BUILDING.

methods in vogue in American cities   There are also presented in
the Town Hall exhibits from various municipalities and countries
of special features connected with streets, parks and public works

The street is 1,200 feet long, and immediately in front of the main
entrance to the Exposition   It is approximately four city blocks in
length, with a public square in the center, and buildings along both
sides of the street   The paving, the parking, and the equipment of
this street are according to improved methods, no matter from what
part of the world obtained, the object being to illustrate the highest
ideals that have been realized along particular lines by the most advanced cities in the world

The buildings along the street are a combination of the utilities
required by the Exposition, such as the hospital, restaurants and the
various exhibit buildings erected by municipalities for the accommo-
dation of municipal exhibits   In the center of the street is the Town
Hall, fronted by the Civic Pride Monument, designed by J Massey
Rhind, of Boston, which faces the public square, laid down in lawns
paths and fountains, and about which buildings of a public nature
might be erected

To the right are the Twin City building of St Paul and Minneapolis and the Guild Hall of Scranton, Pa, and the Model Play-
grounds, where children may be left, to be cared for by a competent
party   A fee is charged   The Board of Lady managers joins in the
support of the play-grounds, contributing one thousand dollars per
month towards their maintenance   Lost children are also looked after
by the matron in charge

Between the Square and the 600-foot main avenue are located
the Kansas City Casino, the San Francisco building, and the New
York City building   At the extreme east end of the street is the Emergency Hospital of the Exposition   A model camp further east is
occupied by the U S Marine Corps

The architectural details of the section have been developed
under the direction of Director of Works Taylor and of Mr Albert
Kelsey, of Philadelphia, Superintendent of the Municipal Improvement Section

LIBERTY BELL

The famous old bell is on exhibition carefully guarded at the
Pennsylvania State building   It was brought here on petition of
75,000 St Louis school children, who wished to enjoy the inspiration
of its presence   Among the bells of the world, no one has been associated with events of as great import to humanity as the Liberty Bell
The original bell was cast by Thomas Lester, Whitechapel, London,
in 1752   It cracked shortly after it was hung and was recast by Pass
& Stow, Philadelphia, April 17, 1753   On July 8, 1776, it proclaimed
the Declaration of Independence to the world   and on July 8, 1835,
rang for the last time   While slowly tolling, during the funeral sol-
emnities over the remains of Chief Justice John Marshall, it parted
through its great side and was silent henceforth, forever   The Liberty
Bell has been removed from the building on four previous occasions—
during the Revolution September, 1777 to keep it from the British,
to the several expositions at New Orleans, January 23, 1885, Chicago,
April 25, 1893, Atlanta October 24, 1895

The Bell is 12 feet in circumference 'around the lip and 7 feet
6 inches around the crown, it is 3 feet following the line of the bell
from the lip to the crown, and 2 feet 3 inches over the crown   It is
3 inches thick in the thickest part near the lip, and $1\frac{1}{4}$ inches thick

LIBERTY BELL.

in the thinnest part toward the crown. The length of the clapper is 3 feet 2 inches, and the weight of the whole is 2,080 pounds.

It is lettered in a line encircling its crown with the sentence:—
"Proclaim LIBERTY Throughout ALL the LAND Unto All the Inhabitants Thereof. LEV. XXV, V, X."

The Bell rests on a movable platform. When it rang for the Declaration, it hung in a heavy wooden frame; the frame was ordered by the Assembly when the Bell arrived in 1753; it was taken down from the steeple with the Bell in 1781 (July 16) and placed in the tower below where it still remains.

During Exposition hours the Bell may be visited at will, no card of admission being required. The sacred relic is guarded by stalwart Philadelphia policemen and is protected by a railing from vandal touch. "Liberty Bell Day" was one of the great events of June, the children turning out en masse to welcome Liberty's messenger. An escort of cavalry accompanied the Bell to its temporary quarters.

QUEEN'S JUBILEE GIFTS.

The greatest array of costly presents ever exhibited to the world were those presented to Queen Victoria on the occasion of her Diamond Jubilee. From the magnificent priceless brooch sent by the Czar and Czarina of Russia to the two pairs of blankets and web of flannel sent by a woolen firm in New Zealand, there was every kind of article produced by man. Some of the most curious and beautiful of these are at the St. Louis Exposition, and were first exhibited in Toronto by special command of King Edward VII., who has sent some special saddlery of a most gorgeous character. They are displayed on the second floor of the Hall of Congresses.

Among the Queen's articles shown here are the famous ivory chair of state, the pair of elephant tusks mounted on a carved ebony buffalo head, the other ivory and ebony articles sent by the great Indian prince, the Maharaja of Travancore. There is a fancy ostrich feather screen from the farmers and women of Cape Colony. There are gold, silver, ivory, ebony, sandalwood and other caskets containing addresses in a hundred different languages, including Chinese, Corean, Malay, Cingalese, Hindoo, and other ancient languages of Asia and Africa. These addresses all exhibit the illuminator's art and what is more important, they testify the love and devotion, not only of the queen's subjects, but of nearly every nation under the sun.

Descriptions of a few of the leading presents are herewith given: A chair of state of elegant carved ivory on truss-shaped legs with lion paw feet, the arms terminating in lion heads, the back enriched with scroll foliage and surmounted by center shell ornament supported by two rampant elephants; the sides and every available part enriched with plaques of covered ivory; the eyes of the lion heads, and several spaces where jewels appear to have formerly been, are

UNITED STATES GOVERNMENT INDIAN SCHOOL.

APOLLO AND THE MUSES—FESTIVAL HALL.

vacant, the seat is inlaid in veined alabaster. A gold and silver tissue drapery round the under side of the frame is finished with tassels and richly chased ormolu ornaments A seat, back and two side cushions are covered with green silk velvet and embroidered in gold and silver thread

A carved ivory footstool with two steps, en suite with the chair of state. The steps are lined with green silk velvet with gold lace border The sides are enriched with movable eagle heads with wing ornaments

A shaped kneeling cushion in green silk velvet, very richly embroidered in gold and silver thread, with two gold and crimson tassels on the front corners Presented by the Maharaja of Travancore

A pair of elephant tusks, mounted on a buffalo head carved in ebony, which is supported on four griffins The tusks are supported higher up by a cross-bar of ebony, and rest on the heads of four figures representing some of the incarnations of Vishnu On the projecting ends of the cross-bar to the tusks are two griffins, with two elephants under them linking their trunks On the center of the bar there is a sixteen-handed figure of Shiva, standing on the prostrate form of an Abamaram or Fiend. All the figures are of carved ebony. From the Maharaja of Travancore

A pair of elephant tusks mounted as flower vases on a stand of rosewood, covered with ivory The tusks are mounted with gold and are entwined by a pepper vine in fruit, worked in gold The vases are supported on two elephant heads carved in ebony, and rising from a base of rock and jungle worked in ivory and elephant teeth. The trunks of the elephants support a lotus of ivory, on which is seated a golden image of Lukeshine, the Goddess of Prosperity From the Maharaja of Travancore

VATICAN TREASURES

The Vatican Treasures are among the most notable objects on view at the Exposition They were sent by Pope Pius X, and are nominally in charge of Cardinal Satolli, as the special representative of the Pope

The collection of the exhibit was under the direct charge of Rev Father Ehrle, Prefect of the Vatican Library, who selected such subjects relating to the Vatican and the present Pope, and his predecessor, as would be most likely to interest American visitors

There are in addition to the relics of Leo XIII and the Pecci family portraits, a death mask and a death impression of the right hand of Pope Leo XIII ; portraits of the present Pope, a series of photographic enlargements showing St. Peter's and the different portions of the Vatican; photographic copies of the most famous decorations of the Vatican, including the Sistine Chapel and St Peter's sketches of the Catacombs and of some famous religious relics and monuments in Rome; a collection of autographs from the archives and the library

A large selection of the work of the Papal Mosaic factory, the most famous in the world, will command attention Replicas of famous classics, which so nearly resemble paintings that a close inspection is necessary to determine their real composition, are shown They are made of infinitesimal pieces of a secret composition, resembling porcelain, which are produced in all the various colors and shades. From a distance they appear to be real paintings, so skillfully are they put together

Reproductions of the Codex Vaticanus, the oldest copy of the Holy Scriptures in existence, dating back to the fourth century. The original is the one from which our Bibles are translated, making it the most valuable book in the world.

Another interesting exhibit is a copy of one of **Cicero's Essays**—de Republica—and many texts and fac-similes of famous classics are included among the treasures.

There are **maps and documents** of great historic value, relating to the missions in the Louisiana Territory.

The exhibit is in charge of Signor Francesco Cogiati, a member of the Ecclesiastical Academy of Arts, and occupies three rooms on the second floor of the Anthropology building.

There is no charge for viewing the treasures. Many of the articles are on sale. The exhibition is one that should not be missed, as this is the first instance of a display of this kind by the Vatican. The Mosaics are notably fine and are entitled to careful inspection.

POWER—By H. Lukemann.
(Palace of Electricity.)

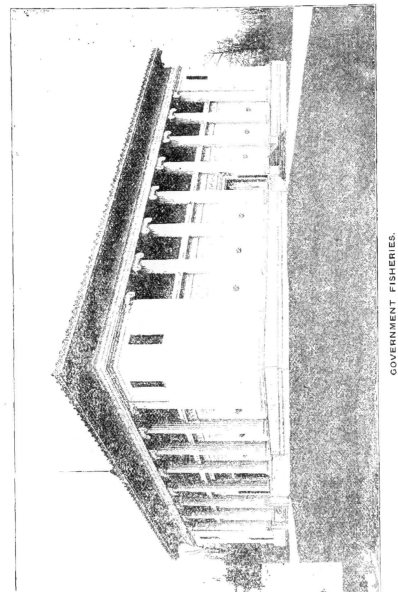

GOVERNMENT FISHERIES.

ELECTRICAL EFFECTS.

In elaborateness and beauty the decorative lighting of the Louisiana Purchase Exposition far surpasses anything ever previously attempted

Nearly 120,000 electric lamps shed their rays at night over the magnificent specimens of architecture and the surrounding grounds which make up the impressive scene that so delights the eye of the visitor. This mass of light makes the grounds of the Exposition as bright by night as by day. The whole picture is bathed in a perfect flood of light Every architectural line or beauty of the buildings is clearly and distinctly brought out by chains of incandescent lamps.

From some points of observation the spectator can behold as many as 90,000 lights at one time, all aglow.

On the Varied Industries Palace alone, 15,000 lamps are shown, this being the greatest number on any one structure on the grounds

About 80,000 lights are used bv concessionaries and exhibitors for decorative purposes.

Charming as are the Cascades and their surroundings in the daytime the sight at night is far more impressive and entrancing It is at this alluring spot that the most profuse display of decorative lighting is made Twenty thousand incandescent lamps are employed in lending brilliancy to the beautiful creation after nightfall

Globes of three colors are used in the illumination, presenting **a** picture that fairly thrills one with its splendor At intervals the lamps are changed for globes of other hues, so that the color scheme of the scene is being constantly varied It is a sight of which one never tires. With each succeeding visit one becomes more and more impressed with its enthralling beauty.

And the grandeur of the picture is heightened by the arrangement of the lights which figure in the gorgeous night view. Under the steps, or ledges, of the Cascades, where the water falls in sheets, rows of variegated lamps are arranged The lights of different hues, forcing their rays through the descending water, give it a beauty and color that surpass in charm anything ever conceived for a World's Exposition The picture is indescribably grand It realizes all our dreams of fairyland

Over the ground are scattered ornamental obelisks, flag poles, lamp posts and bridges, which are gorgeously illuminated by night with incandescent lamps The arches over the bridges are outlined in rows of electric globes; and the architectural beauties of the obelisks, lamp posts and flag poles are splendidly worked out by bands of incandescent lights and protruding brackets

Only incandescent lamps are employed in the main picture of the great Exposition Not an arc light is to be found anywhere It would disturb the evenness of the illumination, which the profusion of incandescent lamps makes brilliant yet uniform

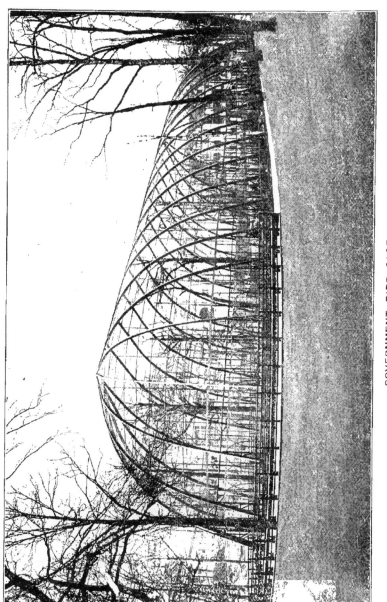

GOVERNMENT BIRD CAGE.

Arc lights are used in abundance along the borders of the 1,240 acres of the Exposition grounds, and on The Pike an arc lamp is to be found at every interval of 75 feet. The grounds surrounding the buildings of the states and foreign countries are also made bright with arc lights.

The stretch of forest land, which is a distinctive feature of this Exposition, has its gloom dispelled at night by a gorgeous sprinkling of arc lights.

Along The Pike decorative lighting is most profuse. Many handsome designs and conceptions are worked out in lamps of varied hues, the whole making a most attractive and gay scene. Some concessionaires use as many as 12,000 lights.

The Missouri State Building has quite an elaborate electric decoration of its own, and some other State buildings have more or less pretentious illuminations.

There is nothing sudden about the turning on and off of the lights at night. First a faint, red glow is noticed in the lamps. Slowly it increases in brightness until all lights on the grounds are finally shown in their greatest intensity. When the closing hour arrives, the lamps are extinguished in the same manner. So gradually is the illumination shut off that one does not notice for awhile that the time to depart has arrived. Almost imperceptibly, the lights grow dimmer and dimmer until eventually only a dull glow is visible. Then the last faint color dies away and darkness envelops all.

The view of the illumination from the lagoons and Grand Basin is particularly beautiful.

AUSTRIAN PAVILION.

PALACE OF VARIED INDUSTRIES AT NIGHT.

TEN DAYS AT THE EXPOSITION.

In order to really understand and appreciate the manifold interests and beauties of the World's Fair, one must spend the entire summer in St Louis; but for the man or woman living within a radius of 300 miles and having but $50 00 to use and ten days' time to spare, a brief survey of the most important features is all that is possible That this may be accomplished with the greatest comfort, the following outing is suggested.

Monday—A lodging place having been previously selected, the morning might be given to making the first visit to the Exposition and observing the general lay-out of the grounds. After luncheon, Palace of Manufactures, 3 hours, Palace of Education 2 hours, dinner at one of the restaurants in the Main Picture; ride in electric launch and observation of illumination

Tuesday—Beginning at 8 a m, ride on Intramural Railroad from Station No 1 to Station No 16 Palace of Liberal Arts, 2 hours United States Fisheries 1 hour luncheon at one of the restaurants in the vicinity, Government building, 2 hours, Mines and Metallurgy, 2 hours, east wing of the Palace of Fine Arts, 1 hour, stopping at German Pavilion on the way, dinner at one of the numerous restaurants on the Plateau, ride on Intramural from Station No. 12 to Station No 1, evening on The Pike

Wednesday—Early walk down The Pike, entering Palace of Transportation from west end, 1½ hours for this building, Palace of Machinery, 1½ hours, Palace of Electricity, 1 hour, luncheon afternoon, Palace of Varied Industries 2½ hours, leisurely walk up the hill, and 1½ hours in west wing of Palace of Fine Arts, dinner and evening on the grounds

Thursday.—Early morning ride or walk to Philippine Village, morning on the reservation, luncheon at Philippine restaurant; afternoon in Palaces of Horticulture, Agriculture, Forestry, Fish and Game, stopping to see the U S Life Saving exhibit and the great Floral Clock, dinner and evening on The Pike

Friday.—Morning among pavilions of Great Britain, China, Belgium, Austria, and the others in the vicinity of the Administration building; luncheon near by, afternoon at Administration group, inspecting Queen Victoria's Jubilee presents the Vatican treasures and the indoor Anthropology exhibit, dinner and view of grounds from Observation Wheel.

Saturday.—Morning on Plateau of States, luncheon and afternoon in the Gulch, and visit to U. S Bird Cage, dinner and evening on The Pike.

Sunday.—The grounds not being open, the day may be spent in the beautiful residence districts and parks of the city

Monday.—Early walk through grounds, 2 hours in American section, Palace of Fine Arts, 1 hour at State and other buildings;

APOTHEOSIS OF ST. LOUIS—By C. H. Niehaus.
(Plaza of St. Louis.)

eaily luncheon and afternoon at Jerusalem, Japan and the State buildings west of the Terrace ot States, dinner and evening in Cascade Gardens

Tuesday—Morning in the Model Street, afternoon on the Mississippi or at Shaw s Garden, one of the finest botanical gardens in the world, evening at a theater or summer garden

Wednesday—Having taken a more or less hasty look at all the principal sights of the Fair, the visitor should give the last day to the buildings in which his interest centers If his taste runs to mechanics, he can find ample material in the Palace of Transportation, Machinery and Electricity If he is in educational work, the Palaces of Education and Liberal Arts will claim his time Should his inclination be towards the beautiful his time could profitably be spent in the Palaces of Fine Arts Varied Industries and Manufactures Or he might devote the last day to the outside Anthropology exhibit the queer people from all over the globe, whose primitive dwellings are located to the north and west of the Palace of Agriculture The evening may be spent on The Pike or on the splendidly illuminated grounds, according to the individual taste of the visitor

Cost of Trip.—The cost of such a trip, allowing liberally for transportation, need not be over $50 00 The visitor who is fond of The Pike can economize on food and Intramural fares, and the launch ride need not be taken more than once On Sunday the cost of entertainment should not be as much as on a day spent within the grounds The railroads, on certain days of each month, sell ten-day tickets to St Louis, within a radius of 300 miles for one fare for the round trip

Room and Breakfast, Daily	$1 00 to $ 1 50	
Car Fare to and from Grounds		10
Luncheon		25
Dinner . .		50
Soft Drinks .		05
Launch Ride or Pike Shows	25 to	50
Intramural		10
Cost per day		$ 3 00
For ten days		$30 00
Ten Admissions .		5 00
Transportation .		12 00
Copy of Official Guide (25c) and sundry other expenses		3 00
Total for ten days		$50 00

General Suggestions—It is very unwise to attempt to do too much sight-seeing at the start or to overtax the energies The time spent in moving about should be increased gradually—The many historic spots in and about St. Louis should not be neglected it opportunity to visit them presents itself —Baggage, sleeping car and ticket arrangements should not be put off until the last moment —The United States section of the Art Gallery is open four evenings a week until 10 o'clock, and the time can be spent most enjoyably in inspecting this great collection of works of art

BELGIAN PAVILION.

EXHIBIT PALACES OF THE EXPOSITION.

The great exhibit palaces of the Exposition are fifteen in number. The names they bear indicate the uses for which they are intended. Their location may be readily determined by reference to the ground plan map in the front of the **Official Guide.** They are described in the order of their classification as departments of the Division of Exhibits

PALACE OF EDUCATION AND SOCIAL ECONOMY.

The Palace of Education occupies a conspicuous position in the center of the main picture fronting west on the Grand Basin, at the foot of the east approach to the Terrace of States and Art Hill. It is entirely surrounded by lagoons, but by means of monumental bridges we gain entrance from the main avenues to the central arches or corner pavilions of the Palace. It faces the Palace of Manufactures, north, and the Palace of Mines and Metallurgy, east. This is the first example in exposition history of an entire building assigned exclusively to exhibits of this department, and in this case the demand from foreign nations, states and cities, industrial schools and colleges for exhibit space has far exceeded the capacity of the Palace of Education. As originally planned, the building was provided with a central court of broad proportions, but this has since been enclosed and given over to exhibits

Architecture—The general plan of the Palace of Education is irregular, approaching a quadrangle. The principal entrances are on the axis of the building and in the form of the Roman triumphal arch. Stately Corinthian columns are grouped in pairs and above the entrance is an elaborate attic, crowned by appropriate sculpture. Above the doors are broken pediments that bear reclining figures. The entrances are connected outside by a colonnade of monumental proportions. This structure may be recognized by its simplicity. The style of the Palace of Education is pure classic

Exhibits.—The Education building contains the general exhibits of the departments of Education and Social Economy. These consist of formal displays of the schools and colleges of the United States and foreign governments

The exhibits are classified in their installation, the public schools of the country being in the north corridor of the Education building, the technical mechanical, agricultural and art schools in the west corridor of the building, the universities in the court, and the detectives in the east corridor of the building. The business and commercial schools, and the publishing and commercial houses connected with education are in the southwest portion of the corridor space. The foreign exhibits are located within the court. The exhibits being those of the foremost nations in educational work, Germany, France and England

Thirty three states of the United States, fourteen nations of Europe Asia and Africa and four American cities are represented. The leading colleges and technical schools of America have exhibits. There is a lecture hall for talks and demonstrations, working exhibits, school room, laboratories etc where pupils and teacher are seen at work are shown

Classes for the instruction of defectives are held daily and attract much attention

No separate building has been erected for the Department of Social Economy; certain exhibits of this department are in the south corridor of the Palace of Education, namely, those relating to the general betterments, public health and charities and correction One of the features is a working hygiene laboratory for bacteriological and chemical tests The municipal improvement exhibits are installed in the Model Street.

Model Street —For description of Model Street, etc, see article on "Special Features of Interest."

Sculpture —Robert Bringhurst, the St Louis sculptor, designed all of the sculpture on the Palace of Education (See article on "Sculpture on Buildings and Grounds")

Architects.—Eames & Young, St. Louis

Dimensions —525 by 750 feet, covering 7 1 acres

Cost —$400,000 00.

PALACE OF FINE ARTS.

The Palace of Fine Arts, the only permanent building on the Exposition grounds is located on Art Hill, directly south of the Terrace of States and 60 feet above the general level Because of its color and architecture, which render it out of harmony with the general scheme of the Fair, it is screened from view by Festival Hall It is a fire-proof structure, consisting of four pavilions, so arranged as to form a letter E

Architecture —The main building, which is designed as a permanent art museum, is built of Bedford stone It is 348 feet long by 166 feet deep At the east and west of this building are situated two wings, each 204 feet long by 422 feet deep They are temporary structures of brick with decorative details in staff In the open area at the rear of the main building and between the wings is the sculpture pavilion, a large building of buff pressed brick with trimmings of staff Around this building are ornamental gardens, fountains and statuary The prevailing architecture of the Palace is the simple Ionic, relieved by a colonnade of the magnificent Corinthian order, that leads up to the main or north entrance.

The Palace is, in several respects superior to those of all previous Expositions It is so constructed that large crowds may move about through its galleries without danger of congestion, and it is all on one floor so that there are no tiresome stairways to climb. There are 134 skylighted galleries and a grand court of international sculpture constitutes the central corridor of the main building The galleries designed for the display of paintings in oil are provided with a top light, the ceiling being constructed of cathedral glass The corridor is flanked by alcoves that are filled with exhibits of architectural and sculptural ornament, which may best be studied in connection with the higher examples of the sculptor's art

Arrangement.—The thirty-two galleries of the main building are given over to American painting and industrial art. The collection of pictures is divided into three groups The first of these is the contemporaneous, or works produced within the past twelve years The second is retrospective such pictures as were painted between the

- 64

year 1803, the time of the acquisition of the Louisiana Territory, and the World's Columbian Exposition in 1893 The last group is a loan collection which is composed of the masterpieces to be found in American galleries, whether public or private

In the separate sculpture pavilion are the works of foreign sculptors only. A number of marble and bronze figures are to be found on the galleries of the building and in the central garden

The foreign exhibits of paintings and applied art are located in the two side pavilions Nineteen galleries of the west wing are filled with French paintings inlaid furniture, wrought metal and other art work The south end of this building, five large rooms with side lighting, is given up to the Japanese collection of carved gems, embroideries, enamel work and wrought metal. There are also some antique Japanese prints that are absolutely priceless

In this building may also be found the exhibits of Belgium, Italy, Spain Russia, Cuba and the Argentine Republic

The largest collections in the east wing are those of Great Britain and Germany. Here also are found the collections sent from Holland, Sweden, Canada and Australia In all these exhibits the pictures are divided into contemporaneous and retrospective work

The walls of the galleries are covered with burlap and brocaded cloth of jute fibre The colors used are such as to give the best background for each style of painting In order to obviate the danger of fire, the cloth is all immersed in a fire-proof fluid The decoration of the walls has been carried out by the commissioners of the nations to which the galleries were assigned, thus doing away with the monotony that the taste of one nation would have produced

Comprehensiveness —In all previous exhibitions of art, a sharp line has been drawn between the so-called "fine arts" and industrial arts The Louisiana Purchase Exposition has established a new order of things, obliterating this distinction and admitting to competition all examples of artistic workmanship, whether their purpose be aesthetic or utilitarian Each nation has been requested to send specimens of its handicraft, and this request has met with a hearty response The visitor who knows nothing about painting and sculpture, but who is interested in wood-carving, wrought metal, architecture, pottery or decorative glass, will find the Palace replete with objects of interest. For the first time in the history of art exhibits the architect may come to the art building to study models of finished buildings and perfect specimens of architectural ornament The devotees of the pyrograph may carry home thousands of artistic ideas in wood and leather burning The china painter may learn what is really artistic in ceramic decoration The collection of paintings is not so large as has been shown at some previous expositions, the space being limited so that each nation would be compelled to send only the cream of its artistic product

Classification —The art exhibit is divided into six general classes The first of these is painting, whether on canvas, wood metal or plaster, and by all direct methods and all media, no mechanical reproductions being admitted This class, in addition to oil and tempera painting, includes drawings and cartoons in water color, pastel and crayon, pyrographic designs and miniatures painted on ivory

The second class comprises etchings, engravings and autolithographs in pencil, crayon or brush

The third class is that of sculpture. This includes figures and bas-reliefs in marble, bronze, terra cotta, ivory or any other material, also medals and carved gems

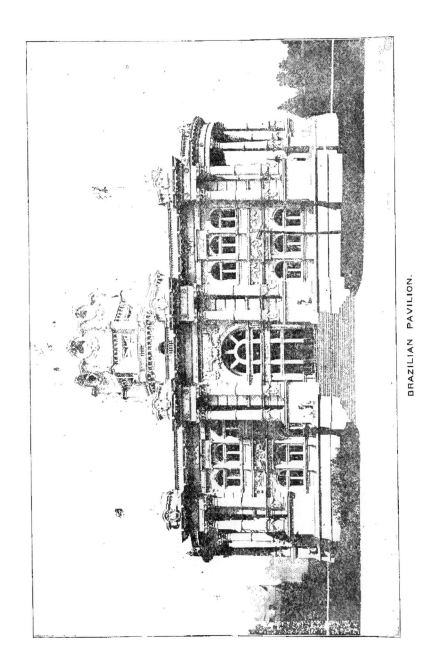

BRAZILIAN PAVILION.

Allied with sculpture is the fourth class, architecture, consisting of drawings, photographs and models of completed buildings, designs of architectural details and mosaics, leaded and stained glass

The fifth class is the loan collection, works of art of any description, selected from galleries whether public or private

The last class is that of industrial art, comprising pottery and porcelain, metal work that does not come under the head of sculpture, artistic leather work, carved wood, book bindings and woven fabrics

For these objects, so far as possible, galleries with side-lighting have been provided The applied art of each nation is exhibited in conjunction with its fine art

Exhibits—The art exhibit more than any other exhibit of the Exposition, is designed to show the composite character of the American people, and the results of European influence and culture The foreign collections of paintings are so arranged that the visitor may study them in relation to our national art, and their effect upon it. With this object in view, the director has placed the American collection in the central building of the Palace of Fine Arts As one passes from the sculpture hall, either to the right or to the left, he enters galleries filled with pictures that are distinctively American These are the work of native trained men, and come as near to "exclusively American" art as has yet been produced

Passing on to the **second tier of galleries** to the west one finds the work of the Americans who studied in Paris, Italy or Spain These show the Latin influence, the training of Lefebvre, Bougereau and Bonnat Crossing over to the west pavilion the visitor finds himself among the pictures that have been the source of inspiration for so many of the younger American painters First in order comes the Belgian section, filling nine galleries This is French art, developed on Belgian soil, and it is utterly different from the art of Holland In this collection the most pleasing canvases are the peasant and animal compositions

In such a collection as that which fills the nineteen rooms that are devoted to French art, it would be difficult to name any works of special interest There are so many marvels of color and line However, he who is looking for "influences" will be compelled to pause before Rochegrosse's elaborate triptych of "The Queen of Sheba before Solomon," in its marvelous frame of wrought metal and gems, and the beautiful composition by L'Hermitte The World's Fair city will doubtless be attracted by LeQuesne's "Founding of St Louis," because of its local interest as well as its intrinsic charm

From the French section one passes through the exhibits of the South American countries that are essentially Latin in their character, to those of Spain Italy and Russia, finally reaching the collection sent by Japan Japanese art is the highest development of the aesthetic in treatment The hard facts of nature are ignored The one purpose of the artist is to produce a beautiful effect This "unrealistic beauty" is not without its effect upon the painters of the Occident American art especially is feeling its influence

Returning to the sculpture hall of the main building, as a starting point, we may study the effect of the widely different Anglo-Saxon ideals and methods upon our painters In the second tier of galleries to the east are installed the works of those men who were trained in Germany, Holland and Great Britain The influence of the Latin and Saxon schools on American painters may be noted in the canvases of Childe Hassam in the west gallery and William Chase in the east gallery Whereas the Latin influence produces delicacy and refinement, the Saxon develops strength and sincerity. The source of this vigorous character may be studied, in the east pavilion, first in the exhibit of Holland, which occupies nine rooms, corresponding with the Belgian exhibit in the west pavilion Marines, landscapes and figures of the peasantry occupy most of these canvases, and in all of them we feel the earnestness, the honesty of the painter Adjacent to the Dutch exhibit are works of the Scandinavian artists, Zorn, Thaulow and the other hardy Norsemen.

In the sixteen galleries that are filled with German art, the Saxon principle is everywhere dominant. Although the Secessionists have no distinctive exhibit, there are many splendid examples of the work of Stuck VonUhde and the band of painters who dared to defy imperial criticism by throwing off the yoke of academic tradition These Secession paintings are a part of the loan collection.

Through the Austrian section and the two galleries that are devoted to these nations that have no special commission one reaches the British exhibit, occupying fourteen rooms Here one may see the masterpieces of Millais, Lord Leighton and Burne-Jones. The best type of painting now produced on British soil is that of the Glasgow men, Paterson, Stevenson, Guthrie and their companions, painting that is much more in sympathy with the German Secession than with the recent art of England

Thus, from the Oriental on one side to the British on the other, the visitor may study the widely different sources of influence that have made American art what it is to-day.

Open at night. The Fine Arts Palace is the only one open at night The American Section is open for inspection four nights a week.

Sculpture.—The Palace of Fine Arts is embellished with a superb mass of statuary, in permanent form on the main building, and in staff, with the same general treatment, along the fronts of the temporary east and west wings. (See article on "Sculpture on Buildings and Grounds ")

Architect—Cass Gilbert, New York

Dimensions—Center, 348 by 166 feet; two wings (each), 204 by 422 feet, total area, 5 2 acres

Cost.—$1,014,000 00.

PALACE OF LIBERAL ARTS.

The **Palace of Liberal Arts** stands at the extreme east of the main picture, near the border of Forest Park It faces northwest on the Plaza of Orleans and southwest on the Sunken Gardens, opposite the Palace of Mines and Metallurgy In this building the dedicatory exercises of the Louisiana Purchase Exposition were held on April 30, 1903 The building as at first planned was provided with a fine inner court, but this feature of the construction had to be abandoned on account of the great demand for space made by exhibitors in this department

Architecture—The general plan of the Palace of Liberal Arts is a quadrangle The main facade on the Sunken Gardens is enriched by three magnificent Roman triumphal arches, one in the center forming the main entrance and two smaller ones near the ends of the facade The arches are connected by a Doric colonnade and the corners are treated in the form of round pavilions The smaller triumphal arches are repeated near the ends of the two shorter facades. The roof is supported by single trusses, spanning the entire exhibit space without columns. The general architecture is of the period of Louis XVI. The building may be recognized by its many triumphal arches and its abundance of ornament.

Exhibits.—The Palace of Liberal Arts contains examples of practically all of the exhibits of the departments. The most important feature, the Grand Organ, is installed in Festival Hall, where it serves for the organ recitals and for accompaniments in the choral concerts. (For description, see Article on "Special Features of Interest.") European nations have made worthy exhibits in the foreign section in the lines of graphic arts, maps, models and plans, books and book-making, public work and surveys, manufacture of paper, chemical, mechanical and scientific instruments, optical goods, artificial textiles, photography, photo-engraving, medals, coins, seals. In the British section

DE SOTO—By E. C. Potter.
(Plaza of St. Louis.)

the working laboratory for the liquification and solidification of hydrogen and the separation of helium, the phosphorescent luminosity of radium, the production of electric crystals, under the direction of the Royal Commission and Professor Dewar, may be seen   Most of the experiments are conducted in a separate building just east of the Model City, but lectures on these subjects are delivered in the lecture room in the gallery of the Palace   Egypt, China and Japan in the foreign section present displays that compare well with those of the European and Southern American countries   Especially noteworthy is China's display of wood carving   The Siamese collection illustrative of the manufacture of paper is full of interest to the student of processes   Japan has a complete newspaper office in operation   Germany's extensive exhibit shows to what a degree of perfection the art of lithographing has been carried in that country.

Domestic exhibits are arranged in classes and mostly illustrate processes of manufacture, such as book-making plants, printing offices, photo-engraving and electrotyping outfits   An equatorial telescope, weighing two tons, is seen in the American section, also a complete lighthouse, a reproduction of Southwest Pass Lighthouse

Architects.—Barnett, Haynes & Barnett, St Louis

Sculpture.—Liberal Arts is the most heavily decorated of the Exposition palaces. A massive quadriga and two flanking groups, which surmount the main triumphal arch entrance on the transverse boulevard, were modeled by Charles Lopez and F. C R Roth, conjointly   This is the most gigantic quadriga ever placed on any Exposition palace   (See article on "Sculpture on Buildings and Grounds ")

Dimensions.—525 by 750 feet, covering 9 1 acres

Cost —$480,000 00

PALACE OF MANUFACTURES

The Palace of Manufactures and its companion, the Palace of Varied Industries, form the most conspicuous objects of the Exposition picture as we enter the main gate   They stand symmetrically on the perimeter of the main picture, one on each side of the Plaza of St Louis and the Grand Court   The two palaces house the exhibits of the manufactures department   the most extensive space ever given by an Exposition to exhibits of this kind   As originally designed, these buildings were to be treated with gigantic towers 400 feet high at the center of the north facades but these were abandoned as impracticable

Architecture —The ground plan of this building conforms to the broken line of the main transverse avenue   The south facade, facing on the lagoon, is ornamented by a succession of deep Roman arches on each side of a colossal Roman niche that forms the main entrance   The smaller arches terminate in other entrances   This same treatment is repeated on the opposite facade   The distinctive marks of this building are the Greek Sphinx, of block pedestals, guarding all the entrances, and the rich cresting on the roof. An open colonnade connects the entrances on the shorter facades, lending a shadowy effect to the design which is most effective   A central court, circular in form, gives a pleasing aspect to the interior   This is treated with a colonnade of fine design in keeping with the exterior

Exhibits —The exhibits of the Manufactures Palace represent two classes of the manufactures department, comprising textiles clothing, embroideries, laces, etc., and hardware, heating and ventilating apparatus, undertaker's goods, and other articles made of wood or metal, in the utilitarian line. Some of the artistic products of manufacture that were crowded out of the Palace of Varied Industries are housed here. The most notable is the collection of Italian marbles and bronzes. France has a magnificent display of imported gowns and fine chinas, and Austria shows a beautiful collection of pottery and glass. Japan has a fine exhibition of silk and silk goods, including models illustrative of the life history of the silk cocoon.

The domestic exhibits cover the entire range of articles assigned to this department.

A unique feature of the Department of Manufactures is the section known as Bazaars or Arcades. These have been designed to cover the requirements of exhibitors who wish to demonstrate and sell their

CANADIAN PAVILION.

wares to the visitor at retail, or for demonstration without sale. There are several of these sections in the two Palaces of the Department, each section divided into booths about 6x6, and the Bazaar has the appearance of a busy department store, in which is carried on the retail business of the Department of Manufactures.

Sculpture.—For the subsidiary entrances of the Palace of Manufactures, Philip Martini has done two marine fountains, one a "Neptune," with trident and chariot drawn by sea horses, the other a "Venus," with spear and attendant horses and chariot. A "Victory," repeated three times, occupies the three niches in the main entrance. In the modeling of this figure the sculptor, Michael Tonetti, employed an electric fan to produce the effect of the wind-blown garments on the partly draped figure. (See article on "Sculpture on Buildings and Grounds.")

Architects.—Carrere & Hastings, New York.
Dimensions.—1,200 by 525 feet, or 14.5 acres.
Cost.—$720,000.00.

PALACE OF VARIED INDUSTRIES.

The Palace of Varied Industries stands opposite the Manufactures Palace, west of the Lindell Entrance, and is on the right of the Plaza of St. Louis as we obtain our first view of the main vista. It was designed in symmetry with the Palace of Manufactures, together with

COWBOY AT REST—By Solon Broglum.
(Grand Basin.)

which it provides space for the exhibits of this department. It was the first building let to contractors. It suffered from high winds during the first winter after its construction, and a 400-foot tower designed for the north facade was abandoned.

Architecture.—The general plan of the Palace provides for an elaborate treatment of the four facades to meet the requirements of its position on the main picture. Its distinctive marks are: **Pairs of towers** above center of south and north facades, and **detached colonnade** in front of south entrance. The south facade on the main avenue is its most striking feature, being provided with an elaborate entrance thrown back behind a circular detached colonnade of majestic proportions An ornate dome overlooks the open court thus formed.

A magnificent corridor passes north through the building from this entrance, breaking at the center into a fine interior court filled with exhibits housed in kiosks and non pavilions

The Ionic colonnade that ornaments the four facades rests on a high base that is broken, between the columns, by arched entrances. Behind this screen-like arcade is a shaded path for pedestrians The square pavilions at the corners are crowned by low domes, and the east and north entrance have graceful towers in the style of the Spanish Renaissance.

Exhibits.—The exhibits in this building are closely allied to the industrial art exhibit in the Palace of Fine Arts, the point of distinction being that in the Palace of Varied Industries the product is shown by the manufacturing firm, while in the Art Palace it is shown by the artist himself Really artistic products that are for sale during the Exposition period are on display in the Palace of Manufactures In the Varied Industries building, an astonishing collection of beautiful things has been brought together The west end is occupied by the exhibits of Great Britain, including a model of King Edward's yacht gorgeously furnished, a model country house, English potteries, Irish laces and a cotton mill in operation; and exhibits of Japan, among which are exquisite embroideries, bronzes, lacquer ware and enameled pottery and metal vases The beautiful Delft ware is noticeable in the Holland, Doulton in the English section and royal porcelain in the sections given over to Denmark The most extensive as well as the most beautiful exhibit in this building is that of Germany. It includes displays of Kayserzinn ware, pottery, tapestries, toys and specially designed rooms, and occupies almost the entire east half of the palace French jewelers show some marvelously beautiful specimens of their art in jewelry and precious stones. In the court Persia displays rugs, carpets and stuffs of native manufacture, and Swiss manufacturers have a building devoted to their peculiar wares

The Floral Clock—(For description, see article on "Special Features of Interest") The Floral Clock is entered as an exhibit in this department

Sculpture.—The sculpture on this building is especially noteworthy. (See article on "Sculpture on Buildings and Grounds")

Architects: Van Brunt & Howe, Kansas City

Dimensions: 1200 by 525 feet, providing 656,250 square feet of space, or 14 5 acres

Cost—$650,000 00

PALACE OF ELECTRICITY.

The Palace of Electricity balances the Palace of Education, from which it is separated by the Grand Basin It is located at the west end of the Terrace of States and Art Hill It presents a fine front to the south facade of the Varied Industries Palace, and on the west is the Palace of Machinery The Lagoon surrounds it entirely, and six bridges connect it with the main avenues The somewhat interrupted effect of the broken line of caves produces a remarkable result when the building is illuminated by electricity, imparting the appearance of lightning.

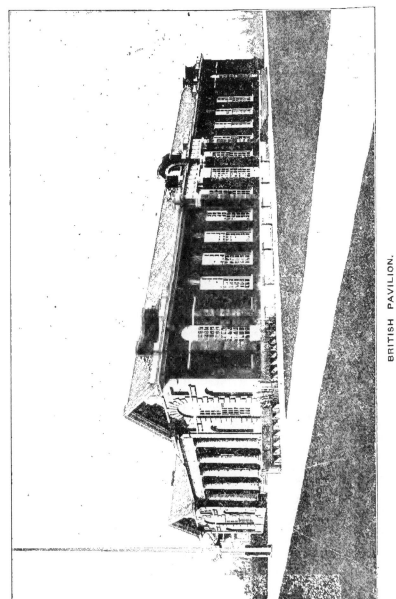

BRITISH PAVILION.

Architecture—The general plan of the Palace of Electricity corresponds to that of the Palace of Education, but there is a central court of wide dimension surrounded by a low, broad inner veranda.

It is constructed for heavy machinery, and a powerful traveling crane, used in the installation of machinery, runs on tracks in the west bay, and the trusses are unusually large and powerful for such a building. On the east side, the columns, grouped in pairs, project far beyond the wall and are connected by a low balcony. Above the colonnade is a beautiful Corinthian cornice. The court pavilions are crowned by pyramidal towers. Surmounting each of these is a beautiful nude figure of a woman, holding aloft a star, by which the building may be recognized.

Exhibits—The exhibits housed in the Palace of Electricity are mostly machines in operation for the generation and use of electricity, dynamos and motors. The largest of these machines are located under the traveling crane, along the west side of the Palace of Electricity, so as to facilitate placing and removing heavy parts. Motor-generators, rotary converters, transformers, rheostats and regulators of every form are so arranged and connected as to demonstrate their various functions. Ingenious applications of motors to the diverse forms of power machines, in which so much progress has been made in recent years, are shown. The principal companies in the electrical industry are mainly interested in this general classification.

Still and working exhibits in the street railway field are shown within the Palace of Electricity, and outside there is a double testing track about 1400 feet long, upon which speed, acceleration, braking and efficiency tests can be made. The phenomena of high potential currents, beyond anything in this line attempted at previous expositions, are shown.

The wireless telegraph and telephone exhibits are among the most attractive features on the grounds. The largest wireless telegraph station ever erected has a conspicuous location east of the Model City. Visitors may send messages by the wireless system between different stations in the grounds, and to other cities having like stations.

The **Radiophone** exhibit, Section 17, shows the transmission of sound over a beam of light. A practical demonstration of the effects of **lightning** on buildings, stacks, etc., is an attractive feature in Section 39.

A visit to the court of the building will reveal the possibilities of **wireless telephony**. One may enter therein and no sound will be heard except those incident to visitors passing to and fro. If a receiver without wires or external connection be held to the ear, the sounds of music or of speaking, foreign to the surroundings, can be distinctly heard. It is like an enchanted court, with a telephone receiver as the magic key.

Practical demonstrations are shown also in electro-therapeutics, electro-magnetism, electro-chemistry, electric lighting, heating and cooking.

There are lamps of every kind, and incandescent lights of every size and color are displayed. Nernst lamps are utilized in lighting one of the buildings, and the Cooper-Hewitt vapor arc lamps are shown in the Palace of Electricity. These lamps emit an intense white light, in which the absence of red rays gives a very peculiar effect. Vacuum tube lighting by means of induced currents is shown. One of the most interesting exhibits is the German laboratory showing the development of chemistry in the past 250 years. Part of the apparatus is from the Museum at Nuremberg. The Liebig laboratory of 1835 is accurately reproduced.

A number of historical exhibits of very great merit are in this building. Thomas A. Edison, Chief Consulting Electrical Engineer of the Department, has a personal exhibit, showing the earliest forms of the incandescent lamp, phonograph, generators and other mechanisms, which he has contributed so much to develop. The storage battery he has designed especially for automobile use, combining light weight with high discharge rates, will draw the attention of engineers as well as the public.

Sculpture.—The six pyramidal towers of the Palace of Electricity are surmounted by repeats of Bela Pratt's group, "Light Overcoming Darkness." The central figure is a nude, holding aloft a star. Figures of "Darkness" crouch at her feet. Farther down on the towers are "Wonders of the Lightning." and "Wonders of the Aurora" by the same sculptor. (See article on "Sculpture on Buildings and Grounds.")

CEYLON PAVILION.

Architects.—Walker & Kimball, Boston and Omaha.

Dimensions.—525 by 750 feet, or 262,000 square feet of floor space, or 9.1 acres.

Cost.—$415,000.00.

PALACE OF MACHINERY.

Location.—The Palace of Machinery is the southeasterly one of the eight great structures which form the central or main group of exhibit palaces. Opposite its north front and across the beautiful Machinery Gardens is the Palace of Transportation. On the south is the Imperial Japanese Reservation and the west approach to the Terrace of States. Its eastern front faces the lagoon and the Palace of Electricity, and on the west is its annex, the Steam, Gas and Fuels building. The palace can be easily identified by its red sloping roofs and its green capped towers. The Steam, Gas and Fuels building, while in its scope embracing more than steam generation, is principally devoted to the boiler plant of the Exposition, and the smokestacks of the boilers will readily locate it. No one who is interested in electric railway or lighting service or in the generation of power should fail to visit this building, which in its entirety (structure and contents) is one of the most consistent and practically educational to be found in the Exposition.

Architecture.—The Palace of Machinery reflects the spirit of renaissance daringly carried out. The German spirit shows itself in the high sloping roofs, backing impressive and profusely decorated entrances. The treatment of the central entrances from the north and east is extremely ornate and deserves careful inspection. The space covered by Machinery Hall is 1,000 feet by 500 feet, with a rectangle cut out of the southwestern corner. The space covered by the

CHINESE PAVILION.

Steam, Gas and Fuels building is 330 feet by 300 feet. Thus the total floor area devoted to exhibits exceeds 12 acres, or approximately five city blocks of the average size. Internally the absence of courts, the high truss lines, the broad concreted aisles, all lend themselves to the proper display of the many imposing and massive exhibits.

Exhibits.—The collection of exhibits in the Palace of Machinery and the Steam, Gas and Fuels building is designed and arranged to exemplify (1) the most modern means and methods for developing, controlling and using power; and (2) the machinery and apparatus used in making machinery of every kind and description. While the two elements are in a sense distinct, yet they are very closely related and the collection of exhibits in conjunction—the one merging into the other—is eminently proper and helpful in presenting to the public examples not only of machinery but of machines for making machinery.

The exhibits illustrative of modern means of generating and availing of power occupy all of Steam, Gas and Fuels building and about one-third of the floor area in the Palace of Machinery. For the main part, these items are in actual service and constitute the power plant of the Exposition. This power plant provides all the energy for lighting the Exposition, pumping the water over the Cascades, for moving exhibits in the various exhibit palaces, for the Intramural Railway and for The Pike shows. The maximum load capacity approximates the power of 50,000 horses. A visitor particularly interested in this topic should begin his investigation at the westerly end of the Steam, Gas

FOUNTAIN OF NEPTUNE—By Philip Martini.
(North Entrance to Palace of Manufactures.)

and Fuels building. There he will find demonstrated the several stages involved in the transformation of the latent heat and energy of coal into either gas or steam. The exhibits in this building illustrate the machinery and apparatus used in automatically delivering, crushing and distributing coal; steam boilers and superheaters; mechanical stokers; mechanical draft apparatus; fire and feed water pumps; gas producers and the various appliances germane to the generation of steam and power gas.

In the western portion of the Palace of Machinery are the engines operated by the steam and gas generated in the Steam, Gas and

Fuels building. While all of these engines are worthy of very careful attention certain of them—as examples of distinct types—should receive particular attention. In the center of the Hall is the Allis engine, which at normal develops power equal to that of 5,000 horses, but has an extreme or overload capacity equal to the power of 8,000 horses. This exhibit represents the most modern and approved type of high power reciprocating engine for central power stations in large cities. In Blocks 44, 49 and 51 are examples of the steam turbine. The steam turbine is the newest development in steam practice. The **steam turbine** is the rotary engine, in contradistinction to the reciprocating, which, for generations, has been the ideal of engineers, but is generally considered almost as much of a practical impossibility as

FOUNTAIN OF VENUS—By Philip Martini.
(North Entrance to Palace of Manufactures.)

perpetual motion. The engines and electric generators operating the Intramural Railway can be distinguished by the red, white and blue posts and rope fencing which surrounds them.

The gas engine exhibits are to the south of the groups of large steam engines. They are extremely interesting in showing the various uses to which the gas engine is applicable in the factory, on the farm and in the home. While in this vicinity the visitor should not overlook the Westinghouse theater with its hourly exhibition of moving pictures and its wonderful lighting effects.

The remaining two-thirds of the Palace of Machinery contains the collection of exhibits illustrative of the modern means and methods employed in making machinery. Here will be found machine tools, covering the entire range of work from a watch to an engine, presses, punches, shears, forge shop equipment, wood working machinery, lifting and conveying machinery, pumps, compressors and hydraulic presses, pulleys, shafting and belting, piping, valves, gauges, meters and accessories used in controlling water, steam and gas. Among the many items of interest one should not fail to see the hydraulic press which uses twice the power exercised in a modern 12-inch rifle when throwing a 1,000-pound projectile over 15 miles; or the machines which grind shafts to within one-five thousandth of an inch of theoretical perfection; or the measuring tools which detect a variation of one-ten thousandth part of an inch; or the machinery

CUBAN PAVILION.

with which a flour barrel can be turned out at a cost of 3 cents for labor.

Among the notable exhibits of this department but installed outside of the Palace of Machinery are the huge centrifugal pumps supplying the water for the Cascades. Each of these three pumps has the capacity to deliver 30,000 gallons of water per minute against a head of 158 feet. The power of these pumps is such that up to the middle of August no more than one of them has ever been in use at any one time. They will be found in the grotto under the eastern approach to the Terrace of States and are well worth a visit.

Sculpture.—The Palace of Machinery is another of the heavily decorated buildings. "Labor and Care" is the subject of the tympanum that is repeated over the six entrances. It is a massive group, with a gigantic male and female figure in the nude, the conception of Fernando Miranda. (See article on "Sculpture on Buildings and Grounds")

Architects —Wideman, Walsh and Boisseliere, St. Louis.

Dimensions —1,000 by 525 feet, or 12 2 acres

Cost.—$510,000 00.

PALACE OF TRANSPORTATION.

The Palace of Transportation completes the main picture of the Exposition on the west It stands at a convenient point for entrance of railroad tracks from the northwest. It presents its station-like front towards the east on the Plaza of Orleans and is a commanding object from every quarter A fine facade also looks north towards the passing trains of the Intramural Railway

Architecture —The general plan of the Palace of Transportation is rectangular and it is the most spacious of the exhibit palaces on the main picture The east and west fronts are provided with three magnificent entrances, embracing more than half of the entire facade, each of the arched openings being 64 feet wide and 52 feet high This is the only building in the group that is not decorated with classic columns. The decorative effect is produced by the use of massive pylons and sculptural ornaments. Above each of the main entrances runs a curving entablature that gives support to colossal figures holding shields The three arches separated by square pylons, form a gigantic porch that is flanked by round towers These are crowned by eagles holding on their backs the hollow, ribbed sphere of the universe, containing the solid sphere of the earth, by which the building may be recognized At the east end 14 tracks enter the building, providing four miles of trackage for the exhibition of rolling stock. The architecture is an adaptation of the style prevalent in France at the time of the Louisiana Purchase

Exhibits.—The exhibits in the Palace of Transportation show the most advanced practice of today in railway building, equipment, maintenance, operation and management, and also the history of the railway as developed during the less than a century of its existence, in all parts of the world Vehicles of all sorts, from the most primitive to the most complex are arranged in the order of their invention and development To give "life" to the exhibits in this department, a testing plant has been installed Various types of locomotives are tested from day to day, the engines traveling apparently at high speed and performing their usual functions, except that they do not move A grand central moving feature is also provided, which is visible from all parts of the building and strikes the eyes of the visitor the moment he enters any one of the sixty doors of the vast structure A steel turn-table, elevated some feet above the level of the surface of the surrounding exhibits, carries a mammoth locomotive weighing over 200,000 pounds The wheels of the locomotive revolve at great speed while the turn-table, revolving more slowly by electric power, carries the engine around continuously Electric headlights on the locomotive and tender throw their searching beams around the entire building This moving trophy, emblematic of the great engineering force of civilization, bears the legend, "The Spirit of the Twentieth Century"

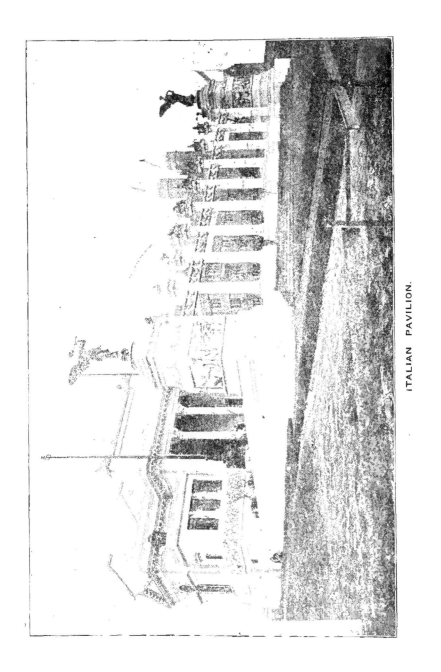

ITALIAN PAVILION.

Other features of importance cover the electrical railway, a comparative exhibit of rolling stock of European, Canadian and domestic railway carriages and models of steamships for ocean traffic, pleasure yachts, electric launches, etc Automobiles and motor vehicles afford one of the most novel and popular attractions of the Exposition A wireless auto for receiving and sending wireless messages while on the road is a novelty The best makers of France, Germany and Great Britain compete with American builders, occupying a vast space with a magnificent display While pleasure vehicles naturally occupy a considerable portion of the space, especial attention is given to heavy motor trucks for general commercial purposes, and to independent motor cars for use on railways

One of the most interesting features is Dr Bircher's War Museum, from Aarau, Switzerland, which illustrates, by relief maps, the strategy of all American wars both on land and sea In the American section of the Marine Division there are full-rigged yachts, boats of all descriptions and a complete historical exhibit of the water transportation of the Mississippi River, also, a model of the port of New Orleans In the German section are presented a model of the port of Hamburg, showing the vessels of the North German Lloyd in dock, and an exhibit by the German Government of vessels and models, evidencing the development of native ship-building Among this collection are shown a number of models of old battleships of the line, and the earlier vessels used by the Hanseatic League The modern methods of transportation in Japan are exhibited in connection with models of her navy yards, docks men-of-war and merchant vessels

Sculpture—The Palace of Transportation has six repeated figures, bearing shields, over each of the triple arches on the east and west fronts (See article on "Sculpture on Buildings and Grounds ")

Architect—E L Masqueray

Dimensions—525 by 1,300 feet, covering 15 6 acres

Cost—$700,000 00

PALACE OF MINES AND METALLURGY

The Palace of Mines and Metallurgy forms the inner part of the east wing of the fan-like plan of the main picture at the Exposition and stands between Government Terrace and Art Hill, opposite the Palaces of Liberal Arts and Education It is perhaps the most remarkable of the palaces being an entirely new departure in Exposition architecture It receives an attention on that account which by reason of its unimportant position it might naturally fail to receive The palace houses part of the Mines exhibits, and the rest are outside the building in the gulch leading southwest into the Plateau of States.

Architecture—The general plan of the Mines building is rectangular, to correspond with that of the Liberal Arts The side walls of the building are set back 20 feet and the extensions are treated with screen effect, affording fine covered promenades around the entire building The base of the screen is adorned with sculpture panels illustrating the operations of Metallurgy and Mining The building is further distinguished by a lavish use of color Four stately entrances pierce the facades, each displaying a pair of obelisks and fine statuary ornamentation. The building is divided into eight oblongs in which there are numerous arcades from 30 to 50 feet wide for the various divisions. A colonnade rotunda marks the center of the building. The architecture is composite, comprising features of the Egyptian, Byzantine and Greek.

Exhibits.—The exhibits in the Palace of Mines and Metallurgy are but a small part of the department. The most imposing feature is the colossal Vulcan, wrought in iron, that presides over the entire indoor exhibit. (See article on "Special Features of Interest.") The building contains the classes which cover all the stages of mining and manufacture of mine products into articles of public and general utility, including the equipment and processes of working mines and ore beds, the extent and development of mineral resources, collections of geology, mineralogy, crystallography, paleontology, ornamental and building stone, machinery for quarrying, handling and cutting stone; gems and precious stones, oils and the processes of handling

JAPANESE PAVILION.

oils. Maps, charts, photographs, etc., of geological and topographical features of mining, and the literature of the subject are also shown. Gold nuggets from the Klondike, securely locked in a stone safe with plate glass front, and lighted by electricity, form an interesting exhibit.

The Mining Gulch, south of the Palace of Mines and Metallurgy, contains working exhibits of this department. This is a natural ravine extending 1,800 feet between Art Hill and the Plateau of States. It averages 400 feet wide and is filled with operating mines and metallurgical exhibits. Placer mines, oil pumps, shot towers, ore ropeways, etc., are shown in their various workings. An aerial railway is installed as a feature of the Gulch.

The Cement Building is an attraction of the Mining Gulch, northeast end. The building is made entirely of cement. In it are exploited the methods of preparing, mixing and using cement and pottery clays An artist's studio and the glazing processes are shown.

Other features of the Gulch are the oil well boring outfits, oil well, a working gold mine and quartz stamp mill in actual operation A typical miner's cabin, hydraulic mining machinery in operation, a New Mexican turquoise mine, copper smelters, a typical Western mining camp, a coal mine working a natural vein of coal with the appurtenances of a modern coal mine are shown in the Gulch

Another of the most interesting and valuable exhibits of the outdoor mining reservation is the plant for testing the coal and lignite resources of the United States This includes full equipment for testing the coal resources, as to their capacity as gas and steam producers and as to their adaptability for cooking and briquetting, etc , and the extent to which they may be improved by washing

In the **Metal Pavilion**, 120 by 125 feet, located in the Gulch, are the operating exhibits illustrating the working qualities of metals, such as zinc, lead, aluminum, copper, tin, etc

A **Model Foundry** pavilion, 120 by 125 feet is installed in the Gulch to illustrate the handling of iron This equipment includes the cupola furnaces and the molds for the melting and casting of iron, and other furnaces and molds for the casting of brass, bronze, etc. There are also in operation electric cranes and other general foundry equipment, including that for finishing, polishing and plating castings of different kinds In one portion of the building, offices and reception rooms have been arranged for the convenience of the foundrymen visiting the Exposition from different parts of the country

Nevada has a **20-mule borax team** as an exhibit, the team making daily trips through the Gulch

Sculpture—The Palace of Mines and Metallurgy is distinguished from its sister palaces by a huge frieze on the colonnade wall (See article on "Sculpture on Buildings and Grounds")

Architect—Theo C Link St Louis

Dimensions—525 by 750 feet, providing 9 1 acres of floor space

Cost—$500,000 00

PALACE OF AGRICULTURE.

The Palace of Agriculture occupies a prominent position on Agriculture Hill, between the Philippine exhibit and University Av , on a part of the site which was added to the Exposition grounds to meet the demands for additional space found necessary as the exhibit department developed This is the largest building ever constructed at an Exposition for a single department, embracing about 24 acres

This building departs materially from the general ornate style of the Exposition palaces since by its position such treatment was not deemed necessary It houses such parts of the exhibits belonging to this department and relating to the development of products of the soil into commercial objects, as the handling of seeds, or of the leaves stocks, etc , and food products and their accessories Outside exhibits far more extensive than ever shown at an Exposition have been installed by this department

Architecture—The general plan of the Palace of Agriculture is a long rectangle The western city limits bisect the building almost equally The four facades are broken by dignified entrances in the form of wide arches, flanked by imposing pylons. Large areas of glass, that take the place of architectural decoration, serve to flood the interior with light. The roof is supported by a great number of enormous trusses resting on posts which mark the aisles. In all, there are seven miles of aisles, but these have been divided to meet the various interests of the department in a way to relieve the fatigue of the visitor.

Exhibits.—The exhibits in the Palace of Agriculture cover all the products of the soil, together with the tools, implements, methods of cultivation, harvesting, irrigation, drainage and the by-products

MEXICAN PAVILION.

of the manufactured forms of these products, their preparation and preservation, including everything edible and drinkable which comes, however remotely, from the soil, and which enters into the home life or commerce of the people of the world Missouri, Illinois and California have particularly fine displays

Special features occupying the central bay are the treatment of corn, tobacco, cotton, cane and beet sugar, pine foods, showing the raw material and the processes and products of their manufacture into commercial form

The dairy section at the World's Fair occupies approximately 30,000 square feet. A model creamery, using 5,000 pounds of milk, is one of the features illustrating processes and will prove of great interest It is equipped with all the latest butter and cheese-making apparatus of to-day and is in daily operation Plate glass encloses it and permits visitors to see every process, and the section is so screened that flies or dust can find no entrance

There is a sanitary milk plant connected with the creamery and a model dairy lunch exhibit where sanitary milk, butter and cheese are dispensed

More than two acres of space are devoted exclusively to foods, including the cereals and their products, tubers and roots and their products, coffees, teas, cocoa, of all kinds and products, refrigerated fresh meats, poultry, fish and game, eggs, farinaceous products, pastes, breads, cakes, tinned meats, evaporated and preserved fruits, spices and condiments, potable waters, beers, ales, wines, brandies, whiskeys, cordials and everything else used as food or drink by mankind

Another great block of space is supplied for the manufacturers of agricultural implements, tools and machinery All the newest and latest devices for the tilling of the soil or the handling of farm products are provided

There is much interest in the foreign section, where England France Germany, Italy, Japan, Mexico Canada, Egypt, Africa and other countries and islands of the sea vie with each other in showing to the new the husbandry of the old world

The cabin occupied by President Roosevelt while residing in North Dakota is an interesting exhibit in this building

Architect —E L Masqueray

Dimensions.—525 by 1,600 feet, or 23 4 acres

Cost —$550,000 00

PALACE OF HORTICULTURE

Architecture.—The Palace of Horticulture stands on Agriculture Hill, 250 feet south of the Palace of Agriculture The structure is in the shape of a Greek cross with a center pavilion and two wings The center pavilion is 400 feet square and the wings are each 204 by 200 feet They are divided from the center pavilion by glass partitions, a difference in elevation which produces a monumental effect Two pleasing minarets flank the north entrance, which is in the form of a triumphal arch The east wing of the building is constructed as a conservatory and furnishes exhibit quarters for specimens of plant culture and for the forced culture of vegetables and fruits The west wing of the building is in use as an exhibit room for horticultural implements In the basement a cold storage plant has been installed and this provides for the care of fruit exhibited in the building Three sides of the west wing have galleries

The center pavilion contains the table exhibits of the pomological department, and here are shown in season fresh fruits and berries in competition. The space between the Horticulture and Agriculture Palaces, and in the ground surrounding them both, is laid out in ornamental rose gardens in which exhibiting florists and nurserymen maintain their respective beds.

Exhibits.—The different states and territories participating in this exhibit made extensive preparations in the way of putting large quantities of fruit in cold storage in St. Louis and elsewhere, so that they were ready at the opening of the Exposition to entirely cover the space allotted to them. The display of fruits is bewildering. Hundreds of varieties of fruits are shown, including every kind grown in temperate, tropical and semi-tropical climates. Nuts are shown in great profusion. Missouri and California are represented superbly and many of the states have very striking exhibits.

Horticultural machinery is shown in the implement room, west wing of the Palace.

GERMAN PAVILION.
(Schloss Charlottenburg.)

Floral Exhibits.—The outside horticultural exhibits are located on Agriculture Hill, on a 50-acre tract of land surrounding the Agriculture and Horticulture Palaces The location is one well suited to the purpose, as it has the necessary slopes and depressions to allow of the best arrangement of the flower beds and aquatic basins and groups of shrubs.

The exhibits are made by the leading nurserymen and seedmen of the country, and cover a large variety of trees, plants, flowers and bulbs. There are planted in this area over 17,000 roses and 100,000 bulbs.

The lakes for the exhibit of aquatic plants cover an area of more than two acres, and in them are shown the rarest and most beautiful specimens in existence

Cut flower displays are shown in competitive contests in season on tables in the Palace of Horticulture

Architect —E L Masqueray.

Dimensions —400 by 800 feet, covering 7 1 acres

Cost —$240,000 00.

LIVE STOCK EXHIBIT.

Live stock has a large section of land on the south side of the Exposition grounds, devoted to exhibits, tests and shows of the live stock section. The Live Stock buildings are located on this tract of about 40 acres, near the Agriculture Entrance The Exposition Company has allotted over $290,000 for awards in this department, and this sum is supplemented by many special prizes. The contests for these prizes call for six great shows, and a concourse is erected on the tract for judging horses, cattle, mules, sheep, hogs, dogs, etc The contests are set according to a program for successive periods of two weeks each, beginning August 23 and lasting until November 19, with just enough time intervening for removal and reception of the departing and arriving breeds The only exception to this arrangement is the demonstration planned to show the dairy and other merits of the cow, which will practically continue through the Exposition period Homing pigeon tests are made from time to time, the winged messengers taking their flight over great distances back to the places they came from The display of saddle, carriage and draught horses is notably good, including many foreign entries from famous stock farms Parades of live stock will take place as follows Horses, asses and mules August 23 and September 1 cattle September 13 and September 22

Numerous barns are located around the concourse for housing the stock on exhibition. There are four model barns for "cow demonstration," to show the dairy and beef merits of the different breeds of cows

A demonstration of **Texas Range Cattle** is set to follow the regular program, at dates after the quarantine period in November

FORESTRY, FISH AND GAME.

The Forestry, Fish and Game building is located south of the Administration group, and west of the Foreign buildings, on the Olympian Way It is the best building ever constructed at an International Exposition for the purposes for which it is designed Its location is admirable, and scarcely a single class of the entire department is lacking in full representation by means of worthy exhibits

A characteristic feature of this building is its central nave, 85 feet wide and 430 feet long, entirely free of posts, and so well lighted that no display is in the least obscure to visitors. The east and west ends of the building are 85 feet wide, 300 feet long, and also free of posts.

Exhibits.—The exhibits of Forestry are partly housed in the building of the Department of Forestry, Fish and Game; but there are many important exhibits of the States and Foreign Governments located in the open air. The building contains exhibits covering historical, illustrative and economical features of forestry and forest products.

The United States Bureau of Forestry occupies a central large location in the west end of the building, and its display covers almost the whole of the first group of the Forestry Department.

The transparencies illustrating forest conditions are conspicuous objects in the building. Other important parts of the indoor exhibit

SIAMESE PAVILION.

comprise a full exposition of the character and extent of Government forest work in the United States.

The outdoor forestry display, while simple, is exceedingly important and instructive from educational and practical points of view. It comprises operations in the management of forest and farm woodlands and methods of economic forest tree planting. A tract of timber of some ten acres carries demonstrations of the principles and practices of conservative forestry, which the Bureau is now applying to public and private timber lands.

Demonstrations of the principles and methods of tree planting for profit on farms, denuded and treeless lands, are shown on a separate tract adjoining the forage and other farm crop exhibits of the United States Bureau of Plant Industry. This tree planting display shows actual practice in the formation of timber farm wood lots and is a most instructive lesson to farmers and others interested in tree planting.

Fish exhibits are installed in an **aquarium**, 190x35 feet, located in the east end of the Palace of Forestry, Fish and Game It has two rows of 60 tanks, arranged on a wide aisle, which communicates through an illuminated grotto with the aquarium, in which the State of Missouri displays black bass, pike, perch crappie, rainbow trout and other well-known food and game fishes A pool occupying the center of the space in this State exhibit contains immense catfish and other characteristic species. Pennsylvania and Alaska also show interesting living fish and game exhibits

A central pool of salt water, 40 feet in diameter, is occupied by the marine fish display of the State of New Jersey For this exhibit natural salt water was brought from the Atlantic Ocean and the Gulf of Mexico Through the courtesy of several of the great railway systems, and as an evidence of their great interest in the Exposition, 60,000 gallons of salt water were transported from these sources free of charge The large game and food fishes of New Jersey were brought in cars from the coast of that State and are to be kept on exhibition during the Exposition period

The Wild Game exhibit of Missouri is shown west of the Palace On a three-acre tract is an artificial lake 200 feet in length, in which living fish and water birds may be seen Around the shores of the lake are enclosures made for deer, raccoon, opossum, squirrel, rabbit, otter, beaver, mink, wild turkey, duck, goose, swan, pheasant, grouse, quail, and other interesting animals native to the State A hunter's lodge contains trophies, literature, hunting and camping equipment On the lake is a platform for fly-casting and other angling tournaments

In the same reservation a **Testing Range**, 50 by 5,000 feet, gives opportunity to show the accuracy of fire-arms, and in the same vicinity a manufacturer of camping equipment displays all the modern forms of tents, together with the appliances necessary for outdoor life

A great collection of historic arms, showing from remote times all the stages of development of the modern breech-loading gun, forms a specially attractive portion of this display It is shown in Section 31 of the Palace

Architect.—E L Masqueray

Dimensions —300 by 600 feet, covering 41 acres

Cost —$171,000 00

ADMINISTRATION BUILDINGS

The Administration group of buildings form part of the future seat of Washington University, an institution of higher education which has long been identified with the development of St Louis They are situated on a tract of land 110 acres in extent and are held under lease from the University Corporation by the Exposition Company. They will be occupied by the University after January, 1905 They have served the Exposition Company for Administration and other purposes since January, 1902

The buildings, ten in number, are disposed in a fine quadrangular plan, on a plateau overlooking the city They are substantially built of red Missouri granite, laid in broken range rubble, with quoins and ornamental courses of cut stone When complete, this will be one of the finest educational seats in America

The principal building is University Hall, used as the Administration building. It stands facing due east, opposite Administration Av, which is the extension of Lindell Bl. With its Tudor-like tower and four-cornered towers surmounting the arched doorway, it forms a magnificent closure to the vista from the entrance to Forest Park, two miles to the east. This doorway is a superb groined vault, 25x38 feet, pronounced by architects one of the best in the United States. A terrace of cut stone, 50 feet wide and 264 feet long, rises to the arched entrance from the level of Administration Av. Busch Hall, the two Cupples Halls and Liggett Hall are built of the same material and in the same style, though not so large as University Hall. They open on a quadrangle in the rear of Administration Hall. Cupples Hall, north side quadrangle, is the exhibit building for the Department of Anthropology. Style of buildings, Tudor Gothic.

Following are the names, dimensions, cost and purposes of the several buildings.

Name	Size—Feet	Cost	Exposition use
University Hall	325x118	$250,000	Administration Building.
Busch Hall	292x100	115,000	Department of Works
Cupples' Hall No 1	263x113	115,000	Anthropology
Cupples' Hall No 2	207x 80	115,000	Jefferson Guard
Work Shop	207x 63	30,000	Service Building
Liggett Hall	90x 63	100,000	Service Building
Power House	120x 50	15,000	Boilers and Machinery.
Library Building	255x144	250,000	Educational Congresses
Gymnasium	94x181 5½	140,000	Physical Culture Exhibits
Southwest Wing	68x306	125,000	Woman's Building

Three of the buildings of the Administration group are used for exhibit purposes during the Exposition period. The Hall of Congresses, west of the Administration building, is the seat of the International Congresses arranged in connection with the Department of Education. Here also are the Queen's Jubilee gifts (see article on same) and back of this building is the one used by the Board of Lady Managers. The Hall of Anthropology (see article on "Anthropology") flanks the Administration building on the north, and at the extreme west of the site are the buildings and grounds of the Department of Physical Culture.

Architects —Cope & Stewardson, Philadelphia

ANTHROPOLOGY

Exhibits of Anthropology aim to represent man as the creature and a worker. The special object of the Department of Anthropology is to show each half of the world how the other half lives, and thereby to promote not only knowledge but also peace and good will among the nations. The department is made up of sections, each designed to illustrate a distinctive and attractive aspect of practical anthropology by means of typical exhibits.

The Ethnological exhibit includes representatives of 23 Indian tribes, a family of nine Ainus, the Aborigines of Japan, seven Patagonian giants and many other strange people, all housed in their peculiar dwellings, such as the wigwam, tepee, earth-lodge, toldo or tent. Among the strangest people assembled are the Batwa pygmies from Central Africa. The various Filipino tribes constitute a complete anthropological display in themselves. (See article on "Philippine Encampment.")

While the living groups form the chief feature of the Section of Ethnology, these are supplemented by notable exhibits of aboriginal handiwork, including one of the richest assemblages of basketry and blanketry extant.

In the north wing of the Administration building is the historical exhibit of the evolution of man, showing the development of weapons, implements and utensils, Egyptian antiquities and mummies, and relics of the Mound Builders and the famous Vatican Treasures. (See article on same.) This building also houses extremely interesting historical displays by the Chicago Historical Society, including letters relating to the Louisiana transfer; Jesuit archives, exhibited by St. Mary's College, Montreal, showing a map drawn by Marquette; Louisiana relics loaned by the French Society of New Orleans; articles displayed by the Missouri D. A. R. and some priceless relics exhibited by the Missouri Historical Society.

In the basement of this building daily tests are given in anthropometry and psychometry. The Queen's Jubilee gifts (see article on same) are displayed in the Hall of Congresses.

NICARAGUAN PAVILION.

The Government Indian School.—The Government has a Model Indian School in a special building, designed for the purpose, situated near the Olympian Way, southwest of the Administration building. The structure is 206 feet long, 77 feet wide, and has a projecting auditorium 30 feet wide and 97 feet deep. Across the east front of the building the young Indians of both sexes, neatly clad, are taught in class rooms, and across the corridor, the old craftsmen ply their primitive trades. There are model cooking schools and dormitories and many curious specimens of Indian handiwork are shown.

Gaily colored tepees and wigwams occupy the space in front of the building and here the adult Indians of the several tribes dwell in true Indian style.

A fine band of Indian musicians renders an excellent musical program at the building daily.

UNITED STATES BUILDINGS AND EXHIBITS.

The United States Government building is a stately edifice, situated on the high ground overlooking the main picture on the east. It faces directly on the transverse avenue and closes the vista in that direction. Its dome, the style of the Parthenon surmounted by a quadriga, is a conspicuous object outlined against the majestic building, erected by the State of Missouri in the background. A grand stairway adorned with statues sweeps to the left of the picture, giving dignity to the composition. The effect is further enhanced by formal beds of herbaceous flowers, clipped hedges and bay trees artistically disposed about the approach.

The hill slope in front of the Government building is terraced with broad stairways, almost completely covering the slope. The building is the largest structure ever provided at an Exposition by the Federal Government.

Architecture.—The ground plan of the building is in general quadrangular. The main facade is marked by a central pavilion with two transverse pavilions, forming end facades. A colonnade of Ionic columns each 5 feet in diameter and 45 feet high, connect the pavilions, forming a portico 15 feet wide and 524 feet long, from which a beautiful view of the Exposition may be obtained. An attic 15 feet in height, richly surmounted with statues, crowns the Ionic order. The height from the bottom of the stylobate to the top of the attic is 82 feet. The dome in the center of the building is 100 feet in diameter, and the top of the quadriga is 175 feet above the ground. The interior floor area is 175 by 724 feet, and is entirely free of columns. The roof is supported with steel trusses 70 feet high and 35 feet apart. To the southwest of the U. S. Government building is situated the U. S. Fish Commission. It is square in plan, 135 feet each way and in general character harmonizes with its neighbor.

POSTOFFICE DEPARTMENT.

Exhibits.—Entering the Government building from the east end, we first see at our left a railroad postoffice car. In it men belonging to the United States Railway Mail Service are actively engaged in "throwing" the mails just as they work while speeding along a railroad track. The mail handled consists of letters and papers mailed to persons connected with the World's Fair, or visitors receiving mail on the grounds, and also the out-going mail. This car is in short, a part of the mail service equipment of the Exposition grounds.

A curious collection of old time relics from the postoffice museum at Washington illustrates the crude beginnings of the postal system. One of these relics is an old-fashioned stage coach that once carried United States mails through a portion of the Louisiana Purchase territory. President Roosevelt who once inspected it examined with a Rough Rider's interest the bullet holes which stage robbers and mountain brigands shot through its stiff leather curtains. Generals Sherman and Sheridan and President Garfield rode in this old coach during the strenuous days of frontier life.

Among the collection of documents showing the primitive postal methods in vogue in the early days of the Republic is to be seen the old book of accounts kept by the first postmaster-general, Benjamin Franklin all written by hand. There is a rare collection of stamps. One of the exhibits is a completely-equipped rural delivery wagon, in which money orders are cashed, letters registered etc. The latest type of mail wagon used in Alaska, pulled by dogs over the frozen snow, invites attention.

Near this exhibit is a collection of photographs of soldiers. These were sent to the **Dead Letter Office** during the Civil War and the Government urges visitors to inspect the collection in the hope that many of the photographs will be identified and returned to the rightful owners. The articles in the possession of the Dead Letter Office constitute an attractive display.

DEPARTMENT OF COMMERCE AND LABOR.

Across the aisle, at the right, is the exhibit of the new Department of Commerce and Labor. Mr. Carroll D. Wright, United States

PHYSICAL LIBERTY—By H. A. MacNeil.
(Main Cascade.)

Commissioner of Labor, had charge of the preparation of the exhibit. The Census Bureau exhibit is made in this section, and the Lighthouse Board shows the great revolving lenses in lighthouses, with other interesting appliances. The Bureau of Standards shows the standards of temperature, weights and measures.

LIBRARY OF CONGRESS.

The space in the projecting northwest corner of the building is devoted to the Library of Congress. A large model of this splendid original building at Washington is a feature of the exhibit. Rare volumes, manuscripts and photographs are to be seen.

SPIRIT OF THE PACIFIC—EAST CASCADE.

SPIRIT OF THE ATLANTIC—WEST CASCADE.

INTERIOR DEPARTMENT.

The next exhibit on the right hand side of the central aisle is that of the Interior Department The Patent Office exhibit belongs to this section There are models of many machines that have borne an important part in the development of the nation's industries. The earliest form of every device of human invention, so far as is possible, is shown We see the actual sewing machine that was the first contrivance of its kind ever constructed; the first typewriter, etc The model of Abraham Lincoln's celebrated device for lifting steamboats off shoals is shown The first harvesting machine, made in the year 150 B C, is one of the most ancient exhibits at the Exposition There is also a model of the first steam engine, made in Egypt in the same year The development of harvesting machines is shown in miniature with some of the machines in operation (Very interesting)

There are daily stereopticon and biograph exhibits and radium demonstrations at 11 a m and 2 30 p m.

The exhibits of the Geological Survey and the panorama of the U S reservation at Hot Springs are noteworthy

Yellowstone Park.—Hundreds of large photographs, taken specially for this exhibit, illustrate the wonders and beauties of the famous Yellowstone Park There is also a moving-picture exhibit. The Yosemite is presented in a series of handsome views

Smithsonian Institute.—Next across the aisle we reach the wonderful exhibit of the Smithsonian Institute The National Museum, on account of its great resources and special facilities, makes the principal exhibit Here are seen the actual skeletons of extinct monsters of many kinds The papier-mache coverings of these models of animals is made from the macerated bank notes that have been redeemed by the Government, incalculable millions in cash being used in the manufacture Amongst the models and the mounted animals are specimens of large game and birds from all parts of the world We also see in this exhibit a great collection of beautiful butterflies and moths from all sections of the globe The collection of minerals is complete and worthy of note.

The children's room at the Smithsonian, which attracted such wide attention at its opening a year ago, is reproduced in this exhibit, with many of the articles which it contains, expressly selected for the interest they have for children This feature of the Smithsonian exhibit has the appearance of a Lilliputian museum, and is attractive not only to children, but to their elders

Meteorites.—A curious and intensely interesting exhibit is a collection of meteorites, some of which weigh many tons The most magnificent collection of minerals in the world is a part of the exhibit of the Smithsonian Tree trunks from the petrified forests of Arizona and Montana represent the forests of ages past, including the great tree ferns belonging to the vegetation of America before man inhabited the earth

Indian Objects—To the aboriginal Indians must be given credit for the interesting display of native pipes, musical instruments, water craft, ceremonial objects, ceramics, sculptures, fabrics and the like, which is to be found here.

Bird Cage.—A mammoth bird cage, located south of the U S Fisheries building, is a never ending source of delight to all interested in the feathered bipeds It is divided into two sections, one for the

NATIONAL WORLD'S FAIR COMMISSIONERS.

Thos. H. Carter. Pres. John F. Miller. John M. Thurston. Jos. Flory. Sec. (Resigned). F. G. Betts. Geo. W. McBride.
(Seated) Martin H. Glynn. Wm. Lindsay. Philys D. Scott. John M. Allen.

large birds and fowl, cranes, storks, pelicans, hawks, swans, pheasants, etc., and the other for the small birds of song and brilliant plumage, of every clime

Indian School.—The Model Indian School (see article on "Anthropology") is part of the display of the Interior Department.

TREASURY DEPARTMENT.

Across the central aisle from the Smithsonian exhibit is the space in which are shown the treasures of the Treasury Of special interest at this Exposition are the old bonds, issued in 1804, in connection with the transfer of the Louisiana territory If we want to learn how money is made, we step into the space occupied by the Treasury exhibit. There we find a set of the machinery used in coining money at the United States mint At 11 a m and 3 p m, daily, Exposition medals are coined here. A most interesting process. The collection of coins is worth an inspection

Health Bureau.—The Bureau of Public Health and the Marine Hospital Service have exhibits in the Treasury section. There is a model showing how a well becomes contaminated with typhoid fever or cholera germs by a neighboring cesspool. Drawings or models of improved tenement houses to replace the unsanitary dwellings of thousands of people in the large cities present an object lesson in civic improvement

Statue of Liberty —We have now reached the center of the Government building, and the statue we observe there is a replica of the splendid and inspiring bronze figure of "Liberty" that crowns the dome of the Capitol at Washington

Life-Saving Service.—The life-saving service has stations on a special lake, east of the Ceylon building The lake is 480 feet long, varying in width from 100 feet to 150 feet and giving a depth of water from 4 feet to 12 feet. Exhibitions in the methods of saving shipwrecked men are given daily at 2 p m by a crew of veteran life savers.

NAVY DEPARTMENT.

Just beyond the main transverse aisle and at the left of the central longitudinal aisle, is the exhibit of the Navy Department The most conspicuous feature of this display is an exact-sized model of an American man-of-war, the battleship Missouri, full size in width, one-quarter in length, with guns and appliances Visitors are free to inspect this interesting model in all its parts Every hour there is an exhibition of biograph motion scenes, illustrative of the life and duties of the crews on United States war vessels, and of the departure of the President, Secretary of War and other officials from the flagship "Kearsarge" after a visit.

There are thirty models of United States naval vessels, also an exact model in miniature of the splendid new buildings of the Naval Academy at Annapolis, which are being built at a cost of $10,000,000

There is a map of the world, 8x20 feet, on which an official of the United States navy will show every day the position of the different ships in the waters of the world.

Dry Dock —A working model of a dry dock, with a floating model of the man-of-war "Illinois," is well worth a visit. The process of

CALIFORNIA BUILDING.

docking a battleship, repairing her hull and floating her, and reverse process is shown at 10 30 a m and 3 p m daily A model floating dry dock is also shown

Marine Corps —The Marine Corps have a model camp near the Model City There is a daily drill of 200 enlisted men. These men have just returned from the Philippines and their camp is intended as an exhibit to show the camp life, hospital drills and tactics of the sea soldiers

WAR DEPARTMENT

Across the center aisle from the navy exhibit is the War Department indoor display Fighting machinery of every pattern is seen here. From the famous old Arsenal, or Armory, at Springfield, Mass , we see a curious collection of weapons one of which is the rifle carried by Jefferson Davis when he was captured

In the War Department's exhibit we see a cartridge-making machine in operation, also a working signal corps telegraph station

Other interesting features are the West Point Exhibit of old flags, guns, etc , and the office wagon used by Gen Geo H Thomas during the Civil War

Models in levee construction, showing how the great levees, protecting thousands of miles of land along the Mississippi river, are made are a feature of the display

A great part of the War Department's exhibit is outdoors, where are mounted big guns for coast defense, and where an army camp is maintained, showing the actual service conditions of the soldiers

Sea-coast defense drills take place daily at the big guns stationed on Government Hill Corps of trained artillerymen are detailed by the U S War Department for this service, and operate the big batteries according to the manual as if in actual warfare, only there is no heavy discharge The guns with their carriages are set on concrete foundations in the quadrangle between the U S Government building and the U. S Fisheries building, east of the Palace of Liberal Arts The carriages are of the disappearing type, and are fitted with all the modern appliances for raising and lowering, transversity, sighting, loading and cleaning, and finally discharging These operations are all performed at stated hours daily The motive power is electricity, and the action is perfect as to mechanism and as to the men behind the guns The foundations with the parapets and machinery are exact reproductions of sections of the coast defenses at Willis Point, L I , and Sandy Hook, N J.

DEPARTMENT OF AGRICULTURE.

Department of Agriculture —The Department of Agriculture, occupying larger space than any other exhibit is on each side of the central aisle, just beyond the War and Navy exhibits A special object of this exhibit is to show what the department is doing to assist the farmers of the United States and to develop our agricultural resources Object lesson roads are shown by the office of Road Inquiry The division of Entomology displays still and live specimens of thousands of insects, destructive and beneficial, native to this and foreign countries, and the plants upon which they prey. The office of Experiment Stations has an exhibit covering the work of the agricultural colleges and experiment stations in the United States, Hawaii, Alaska and Porto Rico. A display of every kind of tobacco grown in this and other countries is made by the Soils Division. Colored and uncolored transparencies to show the forest conditions in different parts of the Government domain are displayed by the Forestry Division. One of the most interesting features of the exhibit by the Bureau of Animal Industry is that showing the inspection of meats, in a practical way, by girl operators.

DEPARTMENT OF JUSTICE

Department of Justice.—In the southeast corner of the building is the exhibit of the Department of Justice. Lawyers find much to interest them in the collection of rare old law books. Everybody is interested in the **autographs of Presidents** Jackson, Lincoln Grant, McKinley and others, attached to pardons. Portraits of the chief justices, from John Jay to Melville B. Fuller, are shown. Specimens of work done by inmates of penitentiaries are exhibited.

DEPARTMENT OF STATE

The Department of State exhibit is on each side of the central aisle at the extreme west end of the building. In this exhibit are many historical relics and documents. One of the documents is the **treaty with France**, transferring the Louisiana territory, which event is commemorated by this World's Fair. Portraits of all the celebrated men concerned in the transaction are shown here.

The sword worn by George Washington in all the battles in which he participated during the Revolutionary War is shown, with several other swords presented to him. In a glass case filled with other relics of **Washington and Lafayette** is a pair of old-fashioned eye glasses, presented to the American general by the French marquis.

The Capitol.—A handsome miniature of the capitol at Washington, 14 by 24 feet, and costing approximately $10,000, is one of the interesting exhibits of the State Department.

BUREAU OF AMERICAN REPUBLICS.

This bureau occupies the Southwest corner of the building. It shows a large relief model of the **Panama Canal** and surrounding territory.

Other features are: A relief map of the proposed Inter-Continental Railway, connecting the U S with the republics of Central and South America, samples of South American products, views of prominent buildings and historic maps, books and documents relating to these countries.

Architect.—James Knox Taylor, Supervising Director, Treasury Department, Washington D C

Dimensions.—250 by 764 feet

Cost.—$350,000 00

FISHERIES.

Passing out at the end of the Government building we see more terraced steps, which lead down to the Government Fisheries edifice, a beautiful structure in the classic Roman style. This building is devoted exclusively to the display and exploitation of the United States Fish Commissioner's enterprises and the exhibition of food fishes and shellfish.

Exhibits.—Around the walls inside the building are 35 glass tanks, in which both salt and fresh water fish are shown. The most interesting of these water inhabitants are the sheepsheads with a full set of teeth; the cow fish with horns and the hippocampus or sea horses. The most beautiful are the myriads of brook and lake trout and the gold fish. Salt water for the sea fish is brought here in tank cars. There is a filter plant, an ice plant and fresh air pump in connection with this display. In the center of this building is a pool, 25 feet square, in which seals and turtles disport themselves.

The actual processes of fish propagation are shown in reality, and others are presented by mutoscope pictures.

Architect.—James Knox Taylor, Supervising Director, Treasury Department, Washington, D. C.

Dimensions.—135 by 135 feet.

Cost.—$50,000.00.

GROUP FOR SIDE CASCADE.

STATE AND TERRITORIAL BUILDINGS AND EXHIBITS.

The **Plateau of States** is an ideal site for forty or more beautiful homes, erected by the various States of the Union. As a rule, these State buildings are merely handsome club houses for the comfort and convenience of the people from the several States. In some, however, displays of the resources of the States are made. The figures given here show the cost of the construction only, exclusive of furnishing and decorating.

Alabama.—Owing to the failure of the Legislature to make an appropriation, it was left to the Commercial Club of Birmingham to raise a fund by popular subscription to make an exhibit of the mineral resources of the State. It thus happens that Alabama has no State building, its only representation being in the Palace of Mines and Metallurgy, facing the south entrance.

The central figure is the huge iron colossus of Vulcan. (For description, see article on "Special Features of Interest".) This is one of the most interesting and striking objects in the entire Exposition. Grouped about the figure are the coals, iron ores, cokes, steel rails, fire and cement clays porcelain clays, glass, sand, etc., produced in the Birmingham district and elsewhere in the State.

Alaska.—Alaska has a group of buildings, just southwest of the Administration building. Fifty thousand dollars was appropriated by Congress for these buildings and exhibits. The main structure, 100 feet in length, 50 feet deep and two stories in height, is colonial in style of architecture, and is flanked on either end by native houses, surrounded by immense **Totem Poles.** Some of these were carved by the aborigines many years ago, while others have been recently retouched and decorated by native artists brought here for that purpose. This unique collection (the first that has ever graced alien soil) was obtained through the influence of Governor John G. Brady, who prevailed upon the natives to donate these highly prized ancestral monuments to augment the attractions of the Alaska exhibit. Blooming at the feet of the giant totems are wild flowers interspersed with shrubs and forest trees indigenous to the country, while the huts themselves are filled with the handiwork of the natives, comprising costumes, utensils, ornaments and curios of all descriptions. Among the most important exhibits is a large collection of minerals, embracing gold, both in quartz and placer, silver, copper, tin, lead and iron. Marble, coal and petroleum are also exhibited, and the display of furs and fishes is unusually comprehensive. Cereals and grasses, vegetables and berries illustrate the wonderful productiveness of Alaska, and a variety of timber is shown in the forestry collection. There is an educational exhibit of the work of pupils of the public and Government schools, a collection of women's work; and an art gallery filled with paintings by Alaskan artists. The halls are adorned with paintings and photographs, interspersed with mounted deer, moose and caribou heads, and a fine collection of mounted birds and pressed flowers.

Arizona.—This Territory's pavilion bears the distinction of being the smallest of the State and Territorial buildings. The building contains three rooms and is one story high. It covers an area 26 by 44 feet and cost $2,500. The amount of money placed at the disposition of the Arizona Board of Managers by the Legislature for Exposition work was $30,000. A splendid showing has been made.

Arkansas.—On one of the highest elevations in the Fair Grounds is the Arkansas building. Broad, sweeping verandas are on all sides where visitors can rest. It is 84 by 100 feet, and cost $17,000.

Native woods, marble and onyx of the State are employed in the building construction. On the walls are photographs of picturesque Arkansas scenery framed in native wood, decorated by Arkansas artists in wood carving.

California.—A replica of La Rabida, an old mission in the southern part of the State, is California's State building. It stands almost in the center of the Exposition grounds on the trail between the Illinois building and Temple of Fraternity. Big arcaded cloisters enter into the construction, which are a marked characteristic of the Californian mission buildings. The architectural mass is concentrated in the center of the structure and consists of two big bell towers, square in plan, tapering upwards in tiers to a lantern-crowned dome.

ALASKA BUILDING.

The area covered by the building is 100 by 140 feet, and the construction cost $15,000. This State has exhibits in the Departments of Education, Agriculture, Horticulture, Mines and Metallurgy, and Forestry.

Colorado.—In all the main exhibit buildings, Colorado has installed representative exhibits. In the Mines and Metallurgy building Colorado ores reveal the State's wealth in minerals. In the Agriculture building a large variety of products of the soil are shown. In forestry, fish and game, timber from mountain and lowland is so treated as to show all of the valuable lumber interests. Many fish from Colorado streams have been transferred to great tanks. This State also takes part in the irrigation demonstration under the supervision of the Agriculture Department.

Colorado has no State building.

Connecticut —The Connecticut building represents the luxurious home of a Connecticut gentleman of the nineteenth century   To produce this result good examples of the period have been studied, and in places, old woodwork, such as the entrance doorway and the woodwork of the large parlor, has been used   Nearly all of this old woodwork was taken from the old Sigourney mansion at Hartford and the Slater house in Norwich, recently torn down

The building has been placed well back from the street, with circular walks and flower gardens in front   The dimensions of the building are 80 by 88 feet, the cost, $40 000   It was dedicated May 3

Georgia —"Sutherland,' the famous home of the late General John B Gordon, situated at Kirkwood, one of the suburbs of Atlanta, is the model of the Georgia State building

The Georgia Legislature made an appropriation of $30,000 to provide for the State's participation in the Exposition, but made no provision for a building   The necessity of one was so apparent that the Commission, with the aid of a committee of citizens raised by private subscription $20,000 for this purpose

Idaho.—Somewhat different from other State buildings is the structure that Idaho has erected   It is one story high and is designed along the lines of a bungalow, with clean cut, plain outlines   The arrangement of the interior is that of a Spanish hacienda, the ten rooms being arranged on the four sides of an open court or patio

The north side of the building is given over to the women of Idaho   The bungalow is 61 by 61 feet in area and cost $8,000   The building was dedicated May 14

Illinois —Facing the broad driveway that winds its way over the picturesque hill, half way between the Plateau of States and the community of Foreign Nations, is the State building of Illinois   A broad veranda surrounds the building on all sides   A square dome crowns the edifice   Gigantic statues of Lincoln and Grant flank the main entrance and on each side of the drum of the dome stand great sculptural groups, symbolical of agriculture and other industries   The ceiling of the State room is deeply paneled   and its walls are ornamented with mural paintings—an epical frieze, 6 feet wide, telling the history of Illinois   The size of the mansion is 198 by 144 feet   It was constructed at a cost of $50,000   The dedication, May 27, was a brilliant affair

Indiana —An up-to-date club building is Indiana's pavilion at the World's Fair   The architecture is of the French renaissance   The building occupies a splendid position in the State group, facing the north and fronting on two of the main avenues   The outside dimensions of the Indiana building are 100 by 135 feet   It cost $31,500   The building was dedicated June 3

Indian Territory —One of the first buildings the visitor sees when he enters the grounds through the State Buildings Entrance is the Indian Territory building   It is two stories in height, covers an area 109 by 72 feet and cost $15,930   Although representing a section supposed to be in the primary stage of development, Indian Territory's building is one of the most dignified of state structures   It is a beautiful Southern mansion in design

Iowa —The first State to erect a building on the World's Fair ground was Iowa   This building is 102 by 148 feet and cost $44,000   At each end is a semi-circular colonnade two stories high

Promenades surround the building at the ground level and on the second story level, about 55 feet from the ground, the latter expanding into big porches

Kansas.—One of the prettiest pavilions on the grounds was erected by the Sunflower State It is two stories high and has a large central hall on the first floor There are three grand entrances The building has a fine location at the junction of three avenues and is but a short distance from the southeast entrance to the grounds It covers an area of 84 by 128 feet The construction cost $29,745.

The Commission has made the finest possible display of the industries and resources of Kansas in stock raising. agriculture and horticulture The mineral exhibit is especially meritorious. It comprises lead, zinc, oil, glass, cement. gypsum and plaster.

Kentucky—The "New Kentucky Home," opposite the Mines and Metallurgy building, covers an area of 138 by 80 feet, including porches and verandas There are entrances on all four sides, emphasized by massive porches, flanked with sculpture groups, symbolical of mines, forestry, manufactures, agriculture and horticulture. The principal feature of the interior is the large reception hall 56 by 60 feet, with hardwood floor. The cost of construction was $29,000. The architecture is colonial.

Louisiana—On a site adjoining that of the United States Government building is a faithful reproduction of the famous Cabildo as it was in 1803, erected by the State of Louisiana. It is furnished throughout with furniture of the time and style of the eighteenth century.

In the reproduction of the Supreme Court room, where the transfers of the Louisiana Territory from Spain to France and from France to the United States were signed, is exhibited a fac-simile of the treaty between France and the United States. signed by Livingston, Monroe and Marbois In the same room are portraits of the signers, together with those of Jefferson, Napoleon, Salcedo, Laussat. Wilkinson and Claiborne. In the courtyard is an original stone filter with the old drinking "monkeys," showing the method of obtaining cool water at that time

In one of the cells of the prison within the courtyard of the Cabildo are the original stocks used by the Spanish in punishing prisoners, which have been removed from the Cabildo at New Orleans The lower room of the Cabildo now used as a City Court, serves as a general reception and reading room where Louisianans are "at home" The building is 95 by 107 feet and cost $22 000.

Louisiana has exhibits in nine buildings, including displays of its three great staples—sugar, rice and cotton, vegetables. raisins, nuts, woods, game and fish Unique features in the Palace of Mines are the Devil in sulphur, and Lot's wife in salt

Maine—A building unique in character, with the motif the log cabin, the walls constructed of logs and the roof covered with shaved shingles, represents the State of Maine on the Plateau of States. It stands in the shady grove that extends from the Pennsylvania building westward to the Gulch On the right of the central hallway on the first floor is located a staircase hall—the staircase constructed of logs and timbers The building is 140 by 68 feet, and cost $20,000. The timber was felled in the Maine forests The building was put together there, taken to pieces and reconstructed in St Louis by Maine woodmen.

Maryland—The Maryland building is on Constitution **Av.**, between West Virginia and Oklahoma The structure is the same as was erected by Maryland at the Charleston Exposition The size of the building is 102 by 50 feet and it cost $20,000

It is two stories high and in the Italian renaissance style There is a terrace at the rear of the building in the wooded land from which a fine view of the Government Bird Cage may be obtained

Massachusetts.—A composition of old colonial mansion style, with many features of historic interest, including in its facade a partial reproduction of the Bulfinch front of the State capitol, and in its interior, reproductions of the old Massachusetts Senate Chamber and the old House of Representatives, with porches at either end similar to those of the old Longfellow house at Cambridge, makes up the Massachusetts building

The rooms are furnished with old heirloom furniture, so precious on account of its history that only State pride induced the owner to part with it temporarily for exhibition at the World's Fair

On the second floor on the main hall is the historical room, with its ceiling carried up into the third story This is well filled with cherished relics and mementos of Massachusetts history. The mansion covers an area 100 by 70 feet and cost $20 000

Michigan—In general appearance Michigan's building, situated opposite the Government Fisheries building, represents a Greek temple It is a two-story structure, built largely of cement on expanded metal, and as material to the value of over $10,000 was contributed, the building represents a total valuation of $30,000 It covers an area 112 by 100 feet The furniture of native woods throughout, was made especially for this building The dedication occurred May 2

Minnesota—A two-story structure, Greek Byzantine in type, was erected by the Minnesota Commission for State headquarters It is decorated with staff ornaments inside and out and has burlap paneled ceilings The furniture was largely furnished by the public schools of St Paul and Minneapolis. The measurements are 92 by 82 feet The structure cost $16,500

Mississippi.—South of the Iowa building and east of New Jersey stands the pavilion used as the headquarters for visitors from the State of Mississippi The building is a copy of Beauvoir, the mansion bequeathed to Jefferson Davis on the gulf coast by Mrs S A Dorsey The President of the Southern Confederacy spent the last years of his life there The outside measurements are 90 by 90 feet and the construction of the building cost $15,000

Missouri—Surmounting Government Hill is a magnificent piece of Roman Architecture, the largest structure on the Plateau of States the home of Missouri Missouri's building consists of three monumental masses connected by balconied links, dome crowned and towering, and profusely decorated with sculpture The dome, a perfect hemisphere, unembellished by a single rib or moulding, is gilded and crowned by a figure representing "The Spirit of Missouri"—a beautiful conceit of the sculptress, Miss Carrie Wood, of St Louis A handsome colonnade of coupled Corinthian columns, each couple of columns crowned with a seated figure, surrounds the drum of the dome This construction surmounts the central mass, at each corner of which is a gigantic sculptured group symbolical of the arts of peace, music, literature, art and architecture The building is completely surrounded on two floors by balconies and porches, which supply an uninterrupted promenade around it at two levels, one 30 feet above the other, and furnish a view of the Exposition from all sides. Another similar promenade 15 feet wide surrounds the dome at the base, 130 feet above the Exposition grounds.

The visitor entering the building finds himself in a gigantic rotunda. 76 by 76 feet, the roof of which is the frescoed soffit of the dome.

An electric fountain in the center of this rotunda spurts water artificially cooled, which cools the surrounding spaces to an agreeable temperature on the hottest day. Passing through the rotunda, the visitor reaches the Hall of State in a wing at the south end of the building. This auditorium is 50 by 75 feet, exclusive of the rostrum, and 40 feet high, with seating accommodations for nearly 1,000 persons. The ceiling is heavily coffered, and there as well as on the paneled walls the mural decorator has exercised his skill. On this floor there are also exhibit halls with observation galleries surrounding them on four sides.

The Governor's suite is on the first floor—the southern rooms

ARIZONA BUILDING.

in the western connecting link. They are furnished in Missouri-grown satin walnut. The Hall of State, or auditorium, is finished in the same material. The western balconied link on the second floor contains the Commissioner's rooms, together with a comfortable parlor for the use of the Commissioners. The eastern balconied link on the same floor contains the hospital and creche and retiring room for women. where they may have the services of nurses and a matron. The building is a temporary structure to be removed after the Fair. It covers a ground area of 366 by 160 feet and cost $105,480. It was dedicated, with imposing ceremonies, June 3.

Montana.—A building exemplifying the strength and grandeur of the State, of modified Doric architecture, represents Montana. It was erected at a cost of $18,000 and covers an area of 124 by 90 feet. The windows and doors are so arranged that the entire building can be thrown open on warm days. The exterior walls are of wood, the studding covered with grooved sheathing on the outside. The sheathing is covered with stucco and colored an old ivory white.

Nebraska —The State appropriation was $35,000. There is no State building, but headquarters have been established at Block 57, main aisle, Palace of Agriculture, where reception rooms, postoffice, lavatories and all conveniences are found Here also is a small theater where free moving picture exhibitions illustrating the various resources of the State are given every half hour In the exhibit rooms of the pavilion is the mounted hide of Challenger, the prize champion fat steer of the world, also a dairy exhibit and a special corn show of over 65 varieties Other Nebraska exhibits are in Horticulture, Education and Mines buildings A large appropriation has been made for the transportation of live stock to the Exposition stock shows.

Nevada.—The Nevada building is of the bungalow type with wide verandas on three sides The State makes its principal exhibit in the Mines and Metallurgy building Gold, silver, copper, lead and precious stones form the basis of these exhibits On account of new and important mineral discoveries lately made in Nevada, the State, feeling a thrill of renewed vigor, has made an unsurpassed exhibit of its resources The wealth of the Comstock lode is exploited here Nevada's building measures 44 by 54 feet and cost $8,000.

New Jersey —Ford's old tavern, at Morristown, which at one time during the war of the Revolution, was General Washington's headquarters, has been reproduced on the World's Fair grounds as New Jersey's State building It stands upon a conspicuous site near the southeast entrance to the grounds The style of architecture is, of course, colonial The minor details in the interior are as faithfully reproduced as are those of the exterior Wall papers of colonial pattern and antique furniture in vogue in Revolutionary days, were specially designed for the several departments. A feature of the main hall is the old-fashioned fire-place and the interesting collection of relics of historic value On the main floor is reproduced the room which was used by Washington as a bed-chamber The building was erected at a cost of $15,000 and measures 63 by 84 feet

New Mexico.—The design of the New Mexico building is in Spanish renaissance The building cost $6,053 It covers an area of 40 by 62 feet, and stands on the main roadway leading to the United States Fisheries building

New Mexico has exhibits in the Departments of Education Mines and Metallurgy, Anthropology, Agriculture and Horticulture The principal exhibit is in the Mines and Metallurgy The Commission has a working exhibit in turquoise mining, and lapidary, showing how the stones are cut, polished and prepared for the market

New York —Situated on the State plaza, with the Kansas, Ohio, Massachusetts and Iowa buildings, all of architectural importance, for neighbors, and overlooking Forest Park is the New York building It is colonial in design and detail, and surmounted with a low dome There is a large hall 60 feet square running the full height, arched and domed in the Roman manner, with galleries around the second story.

No effort has been made in the way of elaborate decoration, but the beauty of the whole depends entirely on the carefully studied detail and architectural lines The building was erected at a cost of $57,000 and measures 300 by 60 feet

North Carolina.—North Carolina exhibits crops of almost endless varieties This State also makes a commanding display of gold, copper and iron and of marbles and building stone, in the Palace of Mines and Metallurgy. In precious stones her exhibit covers a wide range. It embraces diamonds, garnets, beryls, rubies, sapphires, emeralds and rare quality gems

This State has no building

North Dakota.—The Commission decided not to erect a building and to use its appropriation of a little over $50,000 in making exhibits in the Palaces of Mines and Metallurgy, Education, Agriculture, Horticulture and Forestry, Fish and Game The principal display is in the Agriculture building In Mines and Metallurgy, the State shows its lignite and its Portland cement

One of the most interesting features of the North Dakota exhibit is the "Roosevelt Cabin" in the Palace of Agriculture. It is the original cabin occupied for three years, from 1883 to 1886, by President Roosevelt, while a cattle owner in western North Dakota The cabin is arranged as when occupied by the President, and contains numerous articles formerly owned by him

Ohio.—On Commonwealth Av, and within a short distance of the southeast entrance to the grounds, stands the Ohio building The main front of the building faces the west On every side are large forest trees of oak, maple and beach, affording inviting shade Entrance to the main floor is gained by passing between six large columns. The building covers an area of 52 by 188 feet and cost $35,250. It was dedicated with much pomp May 2.

Oklahoma—One of the handsomest buildings on the Plateau of States was erected by Oklahoma The building is two stories high, has an area of 76 by 70 feet and cost $16,000 The front of the building is surrounded by porches on both floors. The structure was dedicated May 23

Oklahoma is creditably represented not only by her handsome pavilion, but also by her displays in the Palaces of Agriculture, Horticulture and Mines

Oregon—This State has reproduced as its pavilion the buildings and stockade used by Lewis and Clark in the winter of 1805-06, known in history as Fort Clatsop This fort was built by the explorers' party at the mouth of the Columbia river on the territory of the Clatsop Indians It was the first building constructed in the Oregon country on the Pacific coast by white men The fort is of primitive style of architecture, one story high and irregular in form It measures 60 by 90 feet, and cost $5,000 Oregon's display of agricultural, horticultural and forestry products is especially noteworthy

Pennsylvania.—The Pennsylvania building occupies a conspicuous position on elevated ground, and is one of the finest in the State group It is 226 feet long, 105 feet wide and cost $75,000 The most imposing feature is a magnificently proportioned rotunda, with a colonnade of Ionic columns Twelve semi-circular arches, each containing an allegorical painting, surmount an entablature of great dignity The color scheme is white and gold There are on the first floor rooms for ladies and one for gentlemen, a reception room, smoking room and package room, where bundles may be checked The second floor has three large 'art rooms" and a retiring room, with an attendant, for the convenience of mothers with their little ones The reading rooms and office apartments are thoroughly equipped for their respective purposes In this building the famous **Liberty Bell** is exhibited. (See article on "Liberty Bell ")

The State is represented in every department of the Exposition

In the Palace of Education the display illustrates the common school system; in Mines and Metallurgy it demonstrates processes of mining, preparing and marketing coal; in Agriculture there is an exhibit of the tobacco, grains, birds, mammals and reptiles; in Fish and Game, a fine collection of live fish; in Horticulture, a display of fruits and nuts.

The Pennsylvania building was dedicated May 2 with appropriate ceremonies.

Rhode Island.—The detail of the interior of the Rhode Island building was taken from the best colonial examples to be found in the Rhode Island plantations. The front piazza, which extends up to the main cornice and forms part of the roof-garden, is in Ionic detail from the old Carrington house in Providence. The circular gable windows are reproduced exactly from the Smith house, where they offered the only examples extant in New England. All the rooms have large open fire-places with gas logs, and their mantels are fine examples of colonial work, loaned to the State by their owners. The building cost $19,000 and covers an area 101 by 61 feet.

ARKANSAS BUILDING.

The building was formally dedicated June 1. This State is represented in the Departments of Education, Horticulture, Fish and Game, Social Economy and in the U. S. Fisheries building. The work of the primary, secondary and normal public schools, and of the various institutions under the control of the Board of State Charities and Corrections, constitute the displays in the Palace of Education and Social Economy. There is a creditable showing in the Palaces of Agriculture and Forestry, Fish and Game. By arrangement with the U. S. Government Board of Commissioners of Inland Fisheries, the State has a special exhibit in the Government Fisheries building, demonstrating the life and culture of the lobster and clam and showing also the enemies of the mollusk. There are numerous exhibitions in the several departments by individuals, firms and corporations.

South Dakota.—The South Dakota building is situated in a beautiful grove of trees, almost directly opposite the structure of Texas and near the crest of Art Hill. The interior of the main hall is covered entirely with a decoration of corn, grain and grasses as the chief agricultural product of South Dakota.

The interior of the building is covered with South Dakota cement in dark tint, with the porches, windows and ornamentation painted so as to relieve the structure from any charge of sombreness This building covers an area of 74 by 86 feet and cost $8,000

Tennessee—The Hermitage, the historic home of General Andrew Jackson, is admirably suited for a State building The style of architecture of the building is the old, dignified colonial, and of ample proportions On the east side of the hall one passes through a cross hallway and views a room that is a copy of the bed-chamber of General Jackson—the room in which he died, January 5, 1845, at the age of 78 Many Jacksonian relics are exhibited in the room The measurements of the building are 104 by 61 feet, the cost $18,000 It stands on the roadway leading to the California building.

Texas.—What one might call the "stellar motif" has been used in designing the building erected by the "Lone Star" State It is an immense five-pointed star, surmounted by a dome of 132 feet from the ground There are, of course, ten walls. At the base, where every pair of walls meet, is an entrance

All the rooms on the second floor are finished in native woods and marbles of Texas The building measures 234 feet from extreme points of star and 144 feet to top of dome It cost $45,516 With great ceremony this building was dedicated Wednesday, May 4

Utah—A cozy club house of modern style of architecture has been erected by the Utah Commission near the State Buildings Entrance The building is 50 by 50 feet It cost $6,000

Utah has an unique display which shows how gold is extracted from the ores A machine built of burnished steel, copper and silver, occupying a space 14 by 30 feet, and entirely covered with a glass case, is the center of Utah's mining display in the Mines and Metallurgy building. Iron and the products of iron are shown in another exhibit Another beautiful display is made of precious stones, including topaz, garnet, ruby and opal

Vermont—The old Constitution House, standing in Windsor, has been reproduced for the State building of Vermont. It covers an area of 50 by 120 feet and cost $5,000 The original building is the house where the Constitution of Vermont was drawn up and signed

Virginia—Virginia is represented among the State buildings at the World's Fair by a reproduction of Monticello (Little Mountain), the home of the President who directed the purchase of Louisiana Mr Jefferson was an enthusiastic student of architecture, and an amateur draughtsman, who brought back from his foreign tours many studies of famous old buildings The plans and specifications for this classic bit of architecture, to the minutest detail in his own hand, are still extant

Millions of patriotic pilgrims will visit the Virginia building who may never see the original home of the illustrious author of the Declaration of Independence, and every American who sees the structure thanks Jefferson's native State for the opportunity. The building covers an area of 113 by 99 feet, and cost $17,000 It has a picturesque site on The Trail leading from the Palace of Fine Arts to the Foreign Section It contains a life size statue of the statesman, contributed by the University he founded

Virginia has exhibits in Agriculture, Horticulture, Mines and

Forestry   Peanuts, pickles and tobacco are extensively displayed   A Pocahontas made entirely of tobacco is a striking feature in the Agriculture building   In Mines there are great figures made of coke, ores, etc   The forestry, fish and game products are noteworthy and cover the whole range of the State's resources in this line

Washington —The State of Washington's building is of unique design   It contributes to a display of the State's lumber resources and at the same time supplies to its visitors a view of the main picture of the Exposition from the observation tower, 100 feet in the air, overtopping trees and adjacent buildings

The building is built entirely of wood, the outside of yellow pine and the inside and the interior finished with the finer grained woods produced by the State   A staircase of native marble is an unique feature   The building is six stories high, towering 114 feet to the base of the flag staff, which rises 50 feet higher   The structure is octagonal in plan, eight gigantic diagonal timbers rising from the ground and meeting in an apex at the observatory line   All the floors are supported on these great diagonal timbers   The building's outside measurements are 77 by 114 feet, and the cost $18,000   It stands opposite the United States Fisheries building

West Virginia —This State erected a building of colonial style with classical domes on the corners and a large dome in the center of the roof, which forms an observatory   There are porches 16 feet wide on the front and sides of the building and one 10 feet wide across the rear   The building was erected at a cost of $18,871   It covers an area of 92 by 108 feet

Wisconsin.—The Wisconsin building is a departure from the ordinary semi-classic style of architecture prevalent in Exposition buildings   The English domestic style prevails   The structure, with its plastered walls and red gable roofs, amid the green foliage, gives a charming effect and is a welcome relief from the generally massive architecture of surrounding buildings   It was erected at a cost of $14,750, and covers an area of 90 by 50 feet   The furniture is of native woods   The building was dedicated May 29

Wisconsin's exhibits are in the Education, Agriculture Horticulture, Mines, Forestry and Machinery departments and cover a wide range   The most important, the Educational, covers branches of school work from the Kindergarten to the State University   In the Palace of Mines there is an extensive display of ores, polished granites and pottery clays   The Forestry display includes a great variety of polished woods   The state is creditably represented by displays of farm products, fruits, live stock and dairy products

Wyoming has no State building   its appropriation of $25,000 being devoted entirely to exhibits in the Palaces of Mines and Agriculture   In the former building, attention is immediately attracted to the State's exhibit of oils   Lumps of bituminous coal, weighing ten tons   of soda, weighing 5,000 pounds, from the natural soda lakes of Albany county, are to be seen   There are specimens of iron running 75 per cent pure and fine copper ore is displayed in abundance   There is also an attractive collection of beautiful stones   Wyoming's grains grasses and fine woods and vegetables and fruits, the latter the product of irrigated farming, constitute the display in the Palace of Agriculture

Porto Rico —This insular possession exhibits specimens of rubber, coffee, dye woods and tropical fruits in the appropriate palaces

ILLINOIS BUILDING.

PHILIPPINE ENCAMPMENT.

The Philippine Exposition was projected by the Insular Government and has cost over $1,000,000. In scope, thoroughness and general interest, it far exceeds any other display on the grounds. It was planned by Secretary of War William H Taft, when he was Civil Governor of the Islands The display embraces about 70,000 exhibits, arranged in over 300 classes and more than 100 groups

The Philippine Exposition is located on a picturesque tract of 47 acres It is in the center of the west section of the main Exposition grounds, a little beyond the Agriculture building Perhaps, the most striking feature of the display is its naturalness There is no attempt at artificiality, no straining after effect More than 1,100 persons are housed in the reservation The native Filipinos are gathered in villages, in houses built by their own hands Here they live, abiding by the customs of their various tribes

An elaborate system of buildings has been erected in the enclosure Special attention has been paid to the landscape and a large lake is at the service of the water Moros and other coast tribes Within the Visayan village alone there is a church, a market, a theater and a municipal building.

The Native Filipinos.—The people of the Philippines have given in this Exposition proof of the high-spirited patriotic pride which in the midst of many difficulties has induced them to make sacrifices, in order that the resources and conditions of their country might appear in a dignified manner before the civilized world. Many of the Honorary Philippine Commissioners now in this country have, as members of the Philippine Commission and as Governors of Provinces, largely contributed to the success of the Philippine display.

As special guests of the Philippine Board, 50 Honorary Commissioners. appointed by the Philippine Government, have come to represent their country in the United States. These representative residents of the islands are making a tour of the United States, investigating its industrial, commercial, social and economic conditions. They have been entertained by President Roosevelt, and by prominent citizens in Chicago, Boston, Cincinnati and other large cities. They will remain for several months in St. Louis to study the Exposition

One hundred selected Philippine students will shortly arrive to study for a number of years in the United States They will come to the Fair and be housed in the Philippine grounds, and serve as guides through the vast Philippine display

Constabulary Guard.—In the spacious cuartel are quartered the Constabulary Guard. the native police-military organization of the Philippines These men are commanded by American and native officers They have a band of 80 pieces Their daily dress parade is one of the novel Exposition sights witnessed by thousands John Philip Sousa said. after hearing a concert by this native band, "I marvel at their skill"

Philippine Scouts—In the rear of the cuartel picturesquely encamped in the forest are the 400 Philippine Scouts, officered by regular army men These men form a part of the United States regular army They are commanded by Major William H. Johnston of the United States army. With this organization is a band of 45 natives. The Scouts also have daily guard mounts, parades and the regular drills prescribed by army regulations

Among these Scouts is one company of Macabebes, who have distinguished themselves from the start as the best soldiers and most loyal subjects in the Islands

Visayan Village.—The Visayan Village is located on the shore of Arrow Head Lake It is enclosed by a picturesque fence of laced bamboo and consists of about 20 houses In these the Visayans live just as they live in their homes in the Islands They are a people of artistic temperament and good musicians In the market are many beautiful articles and fabrics The natives illustrate the manufacture of Jusi, Pina and Sinimay cloth, the making of embroidery, hats, mats, canes and various novelties They have perfected the art of wood-carving to a high degree Methods of fishing and transportation are also represented The women of this tribe are very pretty and there are a number of girls who can speak English—venders of novelties.

The Moros of Mindanao.—Two tribes of Moros are represented The Samal Moros are coast dwellers, pirates and seafaring men. The Lanao people are from the interior of Mindanao Very little is known about the inland Moros, but through the offices of Dr Albert E Jenks, Chief of Ethnological survey for the Philippines, representatives of some of the most savage tribes have been brought here For two and a half centuries these people made life miserable for the Spaniards and the seafaring Samals made frequent piratical expeditions to neighboring islands, sacking villages, looting churches and taking thousands of prisoners It is against the Lanao Moros that General Leonard Wood is now engaged on a punitive expedition for the recent treacherous killing of several officers and 35 men of the Seventeenth Infantry. The Samal Moros have been friendly since American occupation, unlike those of the interior The tribe represented is ruled over by Rajah Muda Mandi It is considered the most intelligent of the many tribes inhabiting the island, and the Rajah in 1895 traveled through Europe and was entertained by Spanish noblemen in Madrid He is wealthy, judged by American standards, and has gathered about him many of the luxuries and conveniences of Western civilization He has the power of life and death over more than 5,000 subjects The hatred between the various tribes of Moros is so intense and so sincere that a special guard is on duty in the villages. It is a violation of their Mohammedan faith for their photographs to be taken, and notices have been posted, notifying photographers of the danger of using cameras about this part of the reservation

The Bagobos—Nipa huts have been built for the Bagobos from Danao Bay, who have just arrived Their costumes are covered with multicolored beads For a primitive race, they have cultivated the commercial and agricultural instinct to a very high degree

The Igorote Village.—Probably the most interesting single feature of the Exposition is the Igorote Village This includes three tribes, the Bontoc, The Suyoc and The Tinguanes The Suyocs are the miners and show their method of extracting the metal from the ore Some of their work in copper is remarkable They have their own rice paddies and sweet potato patch The Bontocs are the **head-hunters.** Tattooing is considered an art by them, and across the chest of several chiefs in the village is recorded the result of their head-hunting expeditions These Bontocs are the **dog eaters**, of whom so much has been written in the newspapers The Tinguanes are the agriculturists and are of a milder disposition The Igorotes are in charge of Governor T Hunt Their religion is a kind of spirit worship

— 118 —

IGOROTE DOG FEAST—PHILIPPINE ENCAMPMENT.

The Negritos.—The Negritos are the aborigines of the Philippines. They are black, squat and kinky-headed. They look like the African negro, but are of smaller stature, low in intellect and primitive in their methods of living They are rapidly decreasing in numbers in the islands and recent estimates place their number at 23,000 The Negritos have no permanent homes in the islands, wandering from place to place in small groups and living on herbs and roots and what game they can shoot. They are very skillful with the bow and arrow. Next to the Pygmies, they are the smallest people in the world.

The Manguianes, occupying a special section of the Negrito Village, are from the Island of Mindoro, and are also an unique race. These people have a peculiar alphabet and are of great interest to the scientist.

Philippine Midgets—The Philippine Midgets, Juan and Martina De la Cruz, are the smallest, fully developed people known in the civilized world. Juan is 29 inches high and 29 years old. Martina is 27 inches high and 31 years old They were born in Iloilo, and their parents were average size people

Arrow Head Lake.—Luguna De Bay, or Arrow Head Lake, is a picturesque sheet of water fronting the reservation. The Moros give exhibitions on the lake of the way they handle their crude craft and how they carry on their pearl fishing The lake is crossed by three bridges, illustrating native architecture, the main bridge being a reproduction of the famous structure over the Pasig, the "Puente De Espana." The reservation is heavily timbered and the forest area forms an impressive sylvan background. The main entrance is through the Walled City, reproducing the Spanish walls surrounding the City of Manila, in which are exhibited relics of the various Philippine wars. An immense number of historic relics make this building an interesting museum

The Education Building.—Fronting the main square is the Education building, a reproduction of one of the most noted native cathedrals In the center of the square is a monument erected to the memory of Magellan, by whom the Philippines were discovered only a score of years after Columbus discovered this country. The square is flanked on all sides by reproductions of well known structures in Manila.

The Game and Fisheries Building, bordering the lake, is a building used for the purpose of displaying the native methods of hunting and capture of game, and the methods of fishing. A superb collection of mollusks is a conspicuous feature of this exhibit

The Forestry Building is really an enlarged native house. It is made of Philippine woods and has a long veranda of bamboo, shaded with coils of rattan. A number of specimens of hardwood are shown, the most valuable of which is naria, often mistaken for mahogany One section of the exhibit in the Forestry building is given up to gutta-percha and rubber. The annual importation of these in the United States since 1892 amounts to more than twenty million dollars Gum-chicle, used in the manufacture of the chewing gum used in the United States, is also shown

The Mining Building contains over 2,000 samples of mineral products of the Philippine Islands, besides the methods of mining, gold-washing and the transformation of the ores into metal and metal work. There is a great abundance of copper ore, gold ore and coal There is also petroleum, sulphur, marble and a kind of kaolin, etc.

The **Agriculture Building** contains at least 10,000 exhibits, show-ing the agricultural resources, the implements used in agricultural work and certain products of agricultural industry, and besides, horti-cultural products, including tropical fruits and vehicles of land trans-portation This also shows the houses, wearing apparel and house-hold articles used by farmers, and every other thing used in agri-cultural life

The **Ethnological Building** contains the most remarkable collec-tion of arms, implements, wearing apparel, adornments and innumer-able objects used in the different tribal life in the Philippine Islands

Hospital —In the Hospital Service building ample provision is made for caring for the sick on the reservation All kinds of medi-cal appliances have been installed, a ward of 50 cots arranged, and provision made for giving the natives who happen to get sick during their stay every comfort and convenience. Trained nurses have been engaged, and the medical corps is in charge of Dr Llewellyn R Wil-liamson, United States Army In the Service building will be located the business offices of the Exposition

Building of Commerce.—The Foreign Commerce and Native In-dustry building represents what was in Manila before America con-quered, an Exposition building In this building, also, a collection of over 4,000 samples of goods, imported to the Philippines, is displayed with full data which will greatly interest the American manufacturer and exporter

There is also a model school conducted by Miss Pilar Zamora She will give exhibitions of the methods of instructing the young Filipinos, more than 225 000 of whom are now regular scholars at Government schools on the island

Manila House.—In the Manila House, many articles of domestic industry are exhibited,—largely the work of women from all over the Philippine Archipelago

Government Building —The Government building represents an imitation of the Ayuntamento Government building of the Insular Government in Manila, and contains choice exhibits of art, liberal arts and sciences and some government displays of the principal insular bureaus. The offices of the members of the board are located on the second floor of this structure

Relief Map —An interesting feature of the reservation is the large relief map made by Father Algue, the Jesuit Priest, who has charge of the Manila Observatory. Father Algue is thoroughly familiar with the geology and geography of the islands He is stationed on the reser-vation His map covers an area of 110x75 feet in the open, and is surrounded by circular plank walk More than 2,000 islands are shown in their proper shape and proportionate sizes Inside the building, from which the wall around the main map extends, are 18 relief maps These show the mines, hot and cold springs, location of tribes and races, forestry and agriculture, and other physical feat-ures of interest in the Archipelago Father Algue also conducts a weather observatory, patterned after the one which he superintends in Manila

Organization —The organization of the exhibit was undertaken by a board of three with Dr William P Wilson, Director of the Phila-delphia Commercial Museum, as Chairman The collection of the exhibits in the Archipelago was in charge of Dr. Gustav Niederlein,

BUILDING A MORO VILLAGE—PHILIPPINE ENCAMPMENT.

of Philadelphia, assisted by his colleague, Mr. Pedro A. Pateino, and the Secretary of the Board, Dr Leon M Guerreio The Exposition Board continues its functions in St Louis, under the Presidency of Dr Wilson, who is in general charge of the Philippine Exposition, Mr. Niederlein looking after the displays as Director of Exhibits Mr Edmund A Felder was appointed Executive Officer

FOREIGN BUILDINGS AND EXHIBITS.

The foreign nations which participate in this great Exposition have made zealous effort to outdo each othei in the erection of characteristic buildings and the installation of their exhibits For the most pait they have chosen fine examples of native architecture familiar to the world through history or literature and their pavilions are thus objects of special interest to every visitor to the Fair They will be found described in detail below

ARGENTINE.

North of Administration building and near the Austrian reservation is located the Argentine Republic national pavilion, a reproduction of the second and third stories of the Government Palace at Buenos Ayres.

The two stories of the building are arranged in suitable apartments to permit of a large central chamber, where receptions and exhibitions may be held, and smaller rooms are provided for the offices of the Commissioners

Furnishings for the pavilion were brought from Argentine, and the decorations are harmonious with the taste and style of that country There are maps and pictures of scenes of the country.

Tropical flowers abound in the gardens.

AUSTRIA.

Distinctly Viennese, and the only sample of the art nouveau among the foreign nations is the Austrian National pavilion, which was first built in Austria, taken to pieces and reconstructed after its arrival at the World's Fair

This, on account of its contents, is one of the most interesting of the foreign buildings, as a large portion of the Austrian art display is housed here

The ground plan of the building is in the shape of a capital T, the wing pointing toward the front On either side of this front wing are gardens and fountains, embellished with a profusion of sculpture. The front of the building is flanked by square towers, 47 feet high, of peculiar design in the style of the art nouveau The entire front is enriched with sculpture

The exterior walls are adorned with paintings of pastoral scenes executed by Austrian artists, and the corner pillars of the wall which encloses the gardens are capped with sculptural figures

Inside the building are 13 salons, one for each of the governmental departments, in which special exhibits are kept. There are relief models of the Government mountain railroads, showing bits of fine scenery along the routes, also a model of the greatest railway bridge in the world over the Isanzo river. Most interesting, however, is the fine art exhibition, showing samples of the "new art." The art galleries show the distinctive paintings of the Polish, Bohemian and Vienna artists' associations and many of the pictures are of a high degree of merit. The work of 46 art and crafts schools is displayed, included in which is a fine array of artistic wood carving.

BELGIUM.

The pavilion erected by Belgium is a piece of old Flemish architecture that commands the attention of all visitors to the Foreign Section. It is conspicuous, because of its handsome exterior mural decorations and a towering dome crowned with sculpture

The structure is built mostly of steel brought from Antwerp. It is of substantial character, and after the World's Fair will be sold

Including the spreading entrance stairways, which project on four sides of the building and supply means of access, the building is 267 by 191 feet

There is not a single window in the pavilion, light and ventilation being secured by means of big monitors in the center of the roof. The exterior wall surface is used exclusively for mural paintings. The grounds about the buildings are used for flower beds and shrubbery. The building contains a variety of interesting exhibits of the factories of Belgium, including some excellent bronzes and ivories and art furnitures. The schools and universities of Belgium make an excellent showing, and the Government has a representative railway exhibit. Very attractive is the collection of the weapons and native products of the Congo country

BRAZIL

Crowned with an immense dome, rising 132 feet above the ground, is the magnificent structure which has been erected at the World's Fair by the Government of Brazil. The building is flanked on the east and west by flower gardens which have been carefully groomed. It faces the Belgian and Cuban pavilions on the north and the Nicaraguan building on the east

Three domes show above the roof line at the top of the second story, the center one of which rises 78 feet. The side domes are flat and are only about 20 feet above the roof. Beneath these side domes are loggias, open to the air

State apartments occupy the entire lower floor together with a collection of agricultural products, especially coffee. On the second floor are the offices of the Commission. Above this, breaking through the roof line, is a light well, 42 feet in diameter, which supplies a view of the outside dome. On the third floor, inside the dome, is a gallery from which visitors may have a view of the functions that take place on the second floor. Above this, another gallery surrounds the dome on the outside, and a view is afforded in all directions

Furnishings made from the hardwoods common to the banks of the Amazon supply the spacious rooms and visitors are treated to delicious cups of coffee produced from the far-famed Brazilian product

CANADA.

Half way between Agriculture Palace and the Forestry, Fish and Game building, and directly opposite the national pavilion of Ceylon, is the Canadian building, a spacious structure, designed on the plan of a club house

Commissioner General Hutchinson's official home is at the Canadian building, and he will serve as host.

More than $30,000 has been expended by the Canadian Government in erecting the building and beautifying the grounds. No exhibits are made in the pavilion, but all of the furnishings are reminiscent of the Dominion. There are numerous paintings and pictures of Canadian scenes, and a representative timber exhibit.

CEYLON.

North of the Palace of Agriculture and near the great floral clock stands the beautiful Ceylon pavilion, which cost $40,000, and is furnished in lavish style with treasured bric-a-brac brought from the far East.

The building is 100 by 84 feet. It has two stories and is surrounded by a gallery. The interior has a court, in which Ceylon tea is served by natives dressed in picturesque costumes, with their hair rolled over large tortoise shell combs.

CONNECTICUT BUILDING.

The building is of **Kandian architecture**, being a reproduction of an ancient and historic **Kandian Temple**, one of the oldest pieces of architecture standing. The panels on the walls are decorated with paintings representing scenes in Ceylon. The building is illuminated by ancient Ceylon lamps and modern incandescents.

A distinguished sculptor was employed to design six statues for the building, namely, a Ratemahatmaya in full Kandian costume; a low country Aratchi or Headman, with high comb, long black coat, gold buttons and sandals; a Colombo Chetly, in full white, with large earrings; a Buddhist priest, fully robed, and two Veddahs, male and female.

Elephants and elephant heads carved out of ebony and ivory, boxes of carved ebony and tortoise shell, Kandian brass embossed trays and lamps, porcupine quill jewel cases and work boxes; a full tea service made of carved cocoanut shells, wooden cabinets, "Chatties" and pots, jakwood rice pounders and pestles, panel carvings like

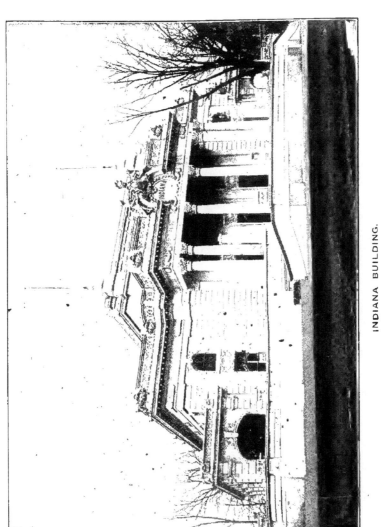

INDIANA BUILDING.

those seen in the ruined cities of Ceylon, and paintings in the Kandian style, representing weird mythological scenes found on the walls of Buddhist and Hindu Temples, are some of the interesting things to be seen inside

Surrounding the building are flower beds where many species of East Indian flora have been transplanted.

CHINA.

Strongly contrasted with its Occidental surroundings is the unique Chinese pavilion, a reproduction of Prince Pu Lun's country seat, with all of its quaint environs The framework was constructed by American workmen, but the delicate carving of the ornamental finish was fashioned by the skilled hands of Chinese artisans, who came all the way from the Flowery Kingdom to apply these last artistic touches

This building erected to hold some of the wonders of the Celestial Empire, stands on Administration Av, midway between the Belgian and British buildings

The woodwork, about 6,000 pieces in all, shows some fine examples of scroll sawing, wood carving, pyrography and inlaying with ebony and ivory

All of this work was done by hand More than $40,000 of the appropriation for the Chinese building was spent for specimens of fine carving with which to make the decorations

Prince Pu Lun's domicile is gorgeous in scarlet, gold, ebony and blue At the entrance to the Chinese building is a picturesque pagoda which attracts attention because of its vari-colored and odd-shaped decorations The pavilion contains some handsome Chinese furniture and porcelains

CUBA.

Typically Cuban is the building representing that young nation It is the reproduction of a well-appointed dwelling house of the present day in the city of Havana, with a tower at one corner which rises to a height of 48 feet

The structure is surrounded on four sides by a 20-foot portico Above is a flat roof, where visitors may promenade on pleasant evenings as they are accustomed to do in sunny Cuba The vista from the top of the pavilion is a splendid one

The interior is divided into three compartments, two offices for the Commission, and a museum and exhibition hall There is also the court, with those fragrant indoor plants typical of the tropics.

FRANCE.

One of the architectural wonders of Europe has been reproduced by France as its National pavilion at the Louisiana Purchase Exposition The historic Grand Trianon at Versailles has been, in effect, transplanted from its historic surroundings to a beautiful plat of ground 15 acres in extent at the World's Fair on Forsythe Av., or the Olympian Way A reproduction of the famous gardens of Versailles is a suitable frame for the historic picture made by the architects in duplicating Le Grand Trianon The building is open to visitors with passes daily, except Wednesday, from 9 a m to 6 p m, and to others on Tuesdays, Fridays and Saturdays from 2 p m to 5 p m

The pavilion consists of a central building, flanked by two wings that terminate each in a pavilion The latter are united by 22 Ionic marble columns, red and green, and the interstices between the windows are adorned by pilasters of the same order and materials

The entire front measures 534 feet. All the apartments are on the ground floor. The roof is surrounded, in Roman style, by a balustrade, ornamented with vases and beautiful groups of figures. A corresponding balustrade extends along the front below, in the center of which is a handsome iron gate opening to the principal entrance. The picture gallery and the billiard room are particularly beautiful. The decorations are superb and the view of the surrounding gardens, from either room, is sweeping.

The Grand Trianon was one of the favorite residences of the great Napoleon. The extensive grounds also contain reproductions of several beautiful chalets of Marie Antoinette.

A broad driveway leads up a gentle slope to the court of the Trianon. It is flanked on either side by raised terraces of sward, and the landscape surrounding the building contains statuary and the most beautiful specimens of the landscape gardener's art. (See article on "Landscape and Gardens.") The right wing has three rooms filled with the exhibits of the City of Paris, including engravings of the masterpieces which decorate the City Hall of Paris. Two rooms are filled with a splendid exhibit of porcelains and bisques from the porcelain factory of Sevres. There is a fine statue of Lafayette by Houdon. The ceilings of the gallerie d honneur, at the rear, are ornamented with three great paintings, typical of Liberte, Egalite and Fraternite. Large gobelins of the period of Louis XIV decorate the wall. There is a salon with some fine vases and examples of art jewelry, glass and email work. Another shows some charming interior decorations, and still another has the exhibit of the Chamber of Commerce of Paris.

GERMANY

Overlooking the main picture of the World's Fair and conspicuous from every part of the grounds is the magnificent structure designed by Emperor William to represent Imperial Germany at the World's Fair. It is on the summit of a large hill, from the crest of which leap the beautiful Cascades and about which are clustered the most important features of the Exposition.

The structure is a partial reproduction of a building renowned in German history, being copied with fidelity from the central portion of the famous Schloss (Castle) at Charlottenburg, near Berlin. The castle was built near the end of the seventeenth century by Frederick I, the first King of Prussia. It was designed by Andreas Schlueter the great German architect of that period.

The architecture of **Charlottenburg Castle** is imposing. The main facade is in two stories. In the center, over the main entrance, towering 150 feet skyward, is an enormous stilted dome. Rooms in the pavilion are furnished with precious old furniture, gobelins and silver ornaments, the products of bygone days. These articles, now owned by the Emperor, have been in the possession of his family for hundreds of years. There is an excellent collection of artistic jewelry and medals of great value, and the wood work and hangings of all the rooms are notable. Surrounding the pretentious building are copies of the famous gardens of Charlottenburg Castle from which plants were taken by the landscape artists to make the likeness more real. A set of chimes, striking the hours in the great tower serves to attract the visitor to the impressiveness of the German file

GREAT BRITAIN.

Most beautiful of the buildings in the gardens surrounding Kensington Palace, where Queen Victoria was born, is the Orangery, an ideal representation of the Queen Anne style of architecture, which has been reproduced in a setting of old English garden as the British National building at the World's Fair.

The Orangery was designed for a greenhouse, and since it was built, 200 years ago, it has never been surpassed as a specimen of garden architecture. It was not only a treasure house for the Queen's choicest plants and flowers, but a place where the Queen and her favored attendants delighted to retire and indulge in quiet conference over their cups of tea.

IOWA BUILDING.

On the occasion of the eightieth birthday celebration, Queen Victoria decided to open to the public the state apartment and the grounds surrounding Kensington Palace, where she was born and where she passed the early years of her life. She was there when her accession to the throne was announced, and it was there that she first met the Prince consort and was wooed by him. The place was filled with pleasant memories and she desired to have the grounds open to her subjects.

The main building at St. Louis is made larger than the original by the construction of wings extending back from either end. In the lower floor are offices and rooms for visitors. In the large room on the second floor is the banquet hall where elaborate functions are held.

The total exterior length of the building is 171 feet and the width

32 feet There are a number of rooms filled with originals and copies of old furniture, arms and decorations of the time of Queen Elizabeth, Queen Anne and King George, as well as a room fitted with modern furnishings

HOLLAND.

Holland's building is on the site formerly allotted to Russia and abandoned by that country when war was begun with Japan The building cost about $5 000 It occupies a space 50 by 40 feet, and shows on three sides steep-pitched Dutch gables with corbie-steps on the slopes It is used for the display of a copy by Hendrik Kleyn, of Rembrandt's "Night Watch," now in the State Museum at Amsterdam An admission fee is charged to view the picture The other parts of the building are free They contain fine antique Holland furniture A typical Dutch garden surrounds the structure

INDIA.

Sombre-like, yet inspiring, is the reproduction of the tomb of Et-mad-Dowlah, which has been made by India at the World's Fair It occupies a site near the Philippine reservation, at the rear of the Forestry, Fish and Game building

This tomb, the original of which is at Agra India, has many of the bulbous dome accessories which have made a world-wide reputation for the Taj Mahal at the same place

In the pavilion samples of tea, coffee and pepper will be served by natives The interior furnishings are typical of East Indian life, and many historic relics hoarded by the ancient races of that country are displayed in the decorations

Plant life as it exists in India is demonstrated in the gardens surrounding the tomb, specimens having been brought from the old-time burial places of India's royalty

ITALY.

The Government of Italy has reproduced at the World's Fair a bit of old Roman architecture trimmed in stately balustrades and affording a garden such as has made artists and poets dream for ages Standing high above the garden level the pavilion is reached by a broad flight of stairs Standards crowned with bronzed Victories tower 100 feet on either side of the entrance The garden which stretches in front of the building is flanked on two sides by a 10-foot wall

Entrance to the pavilion is through a peristyle of Ionic columns. The walls and colonnade are elaborately treated with porcelain entablatures, and are broken at intervals with pylons which carry spouting fountains

Sculpture, rare flowers and all accessories of the building art of the sunny land combine to present a scene most picturesque and beautiful In the main hall are portraits of the King and Queen of Italy, and some sculptures by Monteverde The great electrical genius, Marconi, is given recognition in the pavilion

The Italian building is on sloping ground, south of the Administration building, and opposite the Belgium pavilion, fronting International Av The space occupied is 90 by 150 feet

The pavilion is one-story and shows in the interior a beautiful salon lighted by stained glass windows This is used for Italian concerts Two small rooms where the Commissioners' offices are located connect with the salon The stained glass windows were made in Milan, and the ornamental wrought iron, which occurs in various parts of the installation, is also imported

Pretty effects were secured in painting the pavilion A bronze-colored cresting runs around the building and surrounding the lower structures is a dash of red, being an imitation of terra cotta tiles

The staff work is so artistically executed that the finest marble is imitated and the rarest models of Roman sculpture duplicated

JAPAN

Seven large buildings and a number of small pagodas, built of native material by Japanese artisans, occupy the space allotted to the Mikado's Government, on the site of a beautiful hill west of Cascade Gardens and south of Machinery Palace

The main pavilion is an ornate reproduction of the "Shishinden," a palace at Tokio in which the Japanese Emperor grants audiences to his ministers of state Other buildings, including Commissioner's office, the Bellevue pavilion, a Bazaar a Kinkaku tea pavilion, a Formosa tea pavilion and a tea show building are disposed around the palace Beautiful tiles and carvings have been used in decorating all of the structures, and the furnishings are of the most elaborate and expensive designs

Sloping away from the central buildings are winding walks that penetrate an Oriental garden of great beauty Hidden here and there in the foliage are dainty pagodas The buildings are creations in which American skill took no part They were constructed by clever Japanese artisans brought from the far East for this purpose

Tea being a principal product of that country, beverage made from it by Japanese experts is served in certain pavilions inside the Japanese reservations In other buildings there are on display specimens of the product, and methods of tea culture are demonstrated

MEXICO

Mexico's pavilion occupies a prominent site, fronting 100 feet on Skinker Road (University Bl) and extending west 175 feet It is 50x72 feet in dimension, and the grounds about the structure are used for exhibits of the floral productions of the southern Republic

The pavilion is two stories high and is designed after the style of the Spanish renaissance The windows of the lower story are of stained glass, while those of the upper story are made of photographic negatives, showing cathedrals, monuments, palaces, parks and beautiful bits of scenery in Mexico A very large picture of President Diaz in stained glass occupies a prominent position

On the first floor are a public reception room, reading room, telegraph office and other apartments The second story is given up to rooms for the Mexican Commission and for the press correspondents The glorification of the country's colors is portrayed in a large ceiling picture Mutoscope views of Mexican scenery are presented

In the center of the pavilion is a patio, or court, always a feature of the Mexican building Cacti and plants common to Mexico are used in beautifying the ground

At the south side of the pavilion is a conservatory in which are displayed the tender floral plants of the tropics which cannot be exposed to the St Louis elements

VICTORY—By Michael Tonnetti.
(Main Entrance Palace of Manufactures.)

NICARAGUA

Almost hidden in a garden filled with native plants, the wee Nicaraguan building, smallest in the international group, holds out a welcome to the World's Fair visitors

Designed in the style of the Spanish renaissance, the structure is one typical of the Central American country, rectangular in form and two stories high

With the ever-present patio, or court, it takes on a tropical character noticeable in the pavilions of other Southern countries The lower floor of the building is given to a large hall, suitable for exhibits, and the upper section is divided into a state room and apartments for the Commissioners Flowers brought from the Isthmus have been replanted by native gardeners

SIAM.

Ben Chama Temple, now building in Bangkok, has been reproduced as the National pavilion of Siam, which has an advantageous location between the Mexican and Nicaraguan pavilions

The building is in the shape of a Greek cross, having four arms of equal length radiating from a center. It is crowned by a high pitched roof, with a concave ridge pole This pole' is terminated by the pointed ornament, which is seen on the temples of Siam Each wing of the building has three gables, which rise one above the other, the ridge of each gable being crowned by the ornament mentioned.

The interior, which is decorated in green, vermillon and rich gold, is all one apartment except a small room, 14 by 23 feet, used as the executive office. No posts are in the interior, the roof being carried on Siamese trusses of peculiar construction In the staff decorations the Siamese elephant is used as a motif

Especially beautiful are the quaint Siamese gardens which surround the pavilions.

SWEDEN.

Nestling modestly among the more pretentious buildings about it is a typical Swedish country home of the sixteenth century, brought to the World's Fair in sections and reconstructed to represent King Oscar's Government at the Exposition It is surrounded by its characteristic Swedish garden. All of the material used in the building is from the immense forests of Sweden Even in the furniture provided for the rooms care has been taken to select only that which is in harmony with the home-like surroundings In a niche in the wall is a handsome bust of the King of Sweden, and the walls are decorated with souvenirs of Swedish history and romance. There are samples of potteries from the Gustafsberg pottery, a library of Swedish authors, and pictures of native landscapes. The offices of the Royal Swedish Commission are in a wing of the building

OTHER NATIONS.

Australia will have a display of agricultural products, Ethiopia will show ivory and other products, Morocco is represented by a concession Russia is well represented in several of the palaces. Manufactures, Varied Industries etc Bulgaria, Colombia, Costa Rica. Denmark, Egypt Guadaloupe, Hayti, Honduras, Hungary, New Zealand Paraguay, Persia, Peru, Portugal, San Salvador, San Domingo, Turkey and Venezuela are also represented. Even the principality of Monaco has an exhibit in the Palace of Education.

THE PIKE.

"Cowboys Shooting Up a Western Town" is a typical Western group of statuary, by Frederick Remington at the entrance to The Pike, the amusement section of the Exposition. The frolicsome spirit of this work makes it peculiarly appropriate as an introduction to the lighter merriment of the concessions street. A strong feature of the group is a horse, the hoofs of which do not touch the ground at any point, the animal and rider being supported in the air by contact with the nearest animal companion in the group.

The Pike is story-book land. All creeds and customs are there. Six thousand nondescript characters have stepped from the leaves of history, travel and adventurous fiction to salute you in reality.

Forty amusements, which cost $5,000,000, extend one and one-half miles from the Lindell Entrance west to Skinker Road (University Bl.), turning sharply to the south at that point and continuing in a direct line between the Palaces of Transportation and Machinery on the east and the Foreign Governments' plaza and the Palaces of Agriculture and Horticulture on the west.

Among the attractions is one which cost $750,000 to build, and there are several features on The Pike which cost twice as much as any concession ever yielded at previous fairs. Many of The Pike attractions have theaters and restaurants are to be found in nearly all of them. In some of the theaters there is an extra charge for reserved seats. The prices quoted are for general admission only, but are subject to change from time to time without previous notice. Children are usually admitted for half price.

Starting on The Pike from the Plaza of St. Louis, mountain masses 100 feet high overshadow a Tyrolean village, forming what is known as the Tyrolean Alps. 25 cents.

An Irish village has reproductions of Carmac's Castle, the old House of Parliament at Dublin, and St. Lawrence's Gate. 25 cents.

Under and Over the Sea is a trip to Paris in a submarine boat and a return voyage in an airship. 50 cents.

In the Streets of Seville, senoritas and Rommanys are shown in the Plaza de Toros as seen at Madrid and the quaint market place of Triana. 25 cents.

Hunting in the Ozarks shows the mountain region of Missouri. Game is scared up for the hunter from the natural landscape. Seven shots 20 cents.

Hagenbeck's Zoo, Circus and Animal Paradise shows man-eating beasts in a jungle of growing vegetation, talking birds at liberty, and trained wild animals 25 cents. Circus, 25 cents.

Statisticum, statistics illustrated by moving objects 10 cents.

Ostrich Farm 10 cents.

Temple of Mirth maze and grotesque mirrors 10 cents.

Mysterious Asia is a representation of life in India, Burmah, Persia and Ceylon 15 cents.

Plastic Art is shown in the Moorish Palace, where historic East Indian customs are illustrated 25 cents.

Forty Geisha girls entertain tea drinkers in Japan, with its ancient Oriental temple and replicas of the bazaars of Tokio 25 cents.

A vision of two worlds is seen in Hereafter 25 cents.

Weaving glass into tablecloths and other fabrics is shown in the Glass Weaving Palace 25 cents.

Paris is given up to vaudeville typical of that gay center of fashion and amusement 25 cents.

Ancient Rome is represented by a street of the Augustan period of architecture; vaudeville. 10 cents.

Cairo, reproduction of streets in that famous city. 20 cents.

Creation carries the spectator back to the beginning of time. 50 cents.

Russian Imperial Troupe, from Moscow, in costume, and in native peasant songs and dances. 25 cents.

A history of fashion from the period of the early Roman colonies is shown in the Palais du Costume. 25 cents.

In the Infant Incubator babies are seen through the glass doors of their strange nests. 25 cents.

Old St. Louis, 25 cents. Arena, 25 cents.

Indian Congress and Wild West Show is an assembly of historic tribes of the American Indians and famous scouts. 50 cents.

The Siberian Railroad is an illusion showing a locomotive and train running hundreds of miles through Siberia. 25 cents.

INDIAN TERRITORY BUILDING.

Deep Sea Divers is explained by its name. 15 cents.

The Chinese Village brings one to The Pike joss houses and temples of bamboo. 25 cents.

Eleven sections of the famous Bazaars of Stamboul are reproduced in Constantinople. Theater. 25 cents.

Esquimaux and Laplanders is a view of the life of those people of the Polar region. 25 cents.

The Magic Whirlpool is a descent by boat around a circular waterfall. 15 cents.

The Cliff Dwellers is a duplicate of a section of the caves in the stone age in the Mancos Canyon, Colorado. Indian Dances. 25 cents.

Battle Abbey is a cycloramic reproduction of the battle history of America. 25 cents.

The Naval Exhibit shows a modern sea fight. 25 cents.

Beautiful Jim Key is an educated horse. 25 cents.

Ante-bellum days in the South are revived in the Old Plantation. 15 cents.

The great disaster which overwhelmed Galveston in September, 1900, is reproduced in the Galveston Flood   25 cents.

Hale's Fire Fighters is an exhibition of extinguishing a burning building and saving lives   25 cents.

New York to the North Pole is an illusion of a trip by vessel to the Polar region   25 cents

Wireless Telegraphy is the exhibit of a wireless telegraph company, messages being sent from a tower 200 feet high   25 cents

Jerusalem is a remarkable open air representation of the Holy City   It covers 11 acres and contains 300 houses and 22 streets. Reproductions of the Mosque of Omar, the Church of the Holy Sepulchre, the Jews' Wailing Place, the Via Dolorosa with the Nine Stations of the Cross, are shown   25 cents.

Observation Wheel is a huge steel structure reaching 250 feet in the air and giving passengers in its car a bird's-eye view of the Exposition   50 cents

Miniature railway affords a ride in a perfectly equipped railroad train of reduced dimensions   10 cents.

Boer War; battles between Boers and British   Life in the Transvaal.   25 cents to $1 00

Poultry Farm, 25 cents, "Fairyland," Shoot the Chutes, 10 cents, Scenic Railway, 10 cents, Golden Chariots (merry-go-round), 10 cents, Spectatorium (biophone), moving pictures, 10 cents   Palmistry, 25 cents, and Camera Obscura 10 cents, are additional attractions

FRATERNAL AND SPECIAL BUILDINGS

In addition to the exhibit palaces, State and foreign buildings, and the structures on The Pike, there are quite a number of buildings on the grounds which have been erected by fraternal and other organizations

T. P. A. Building.—Headquarters for members of the Travelers' Protective Association and their friends are at the T P A building on the Plateau of States, between the State buildings of Washington and Louisiana   It has a large central hall for receptions, lounging toilet and other rooms   The $20,000 which the building and furnishings cost was raised by members of the T P. A

House of Hoo-Hoo.—A lumberman's club house built by the Concatenated Order of Hoo-Hoo, and situated near the German pavilion, was destroyed by fire June 24 and rebuilt   It is made up of native woods, 20 varieties being used, with veneers, showing 139 different effects

Temple of Fraternity.—The Temple of Fraternity is an imposing structure of Grecian design, modeled after the ancient Parthenon   It is situated on the summit of a beautiful hill in the central section of the grounds, being surrounded by flower beds and great elm trees   It is three stories high with basement, and contains 40 well-appointed rooms   On the first floor is a Hall of Fame in which are portraits of persons prominent in fraternal work   The Temple is the headquarters of fraternal societies   It cost $62 000

Disciples of Christ Chapel.—An enlarged reproduction of the first chapel built by the Disciples of Christ stands on one of the main boulevards of the Plateau of States, not far from the Grant cabin   It is used as a place of worship and as headquarters for visiting members of that church   The building is hexagon   The original chapel designed by Alexander Campbell, founder of the denomination, was built near Bethany, W Va , in 1840

Woman's Anchorage.—Next to lntramural Station No. 1, north of Palace of Varied lndustries, a house of rest conducted jointly by the Woman's Christian Temperance Union, National Council of Women, The King's Daughters, Monticello Alumnae (Godfrey, Ill.) and Baptist Missionary Society. The Kappa Kappa Gamma Society, a college sorority, also has quarters here. Each society has one or more rooms for the entertainment of its members. Tired people are made welcome. There are toilet and other accessories.

AIRSHIP CONTESTS.

Recognizing the progress made toward solving the problems of aerial navigation, and the possibility, if not the probability, of remarkable achievements in the air, the Exposition has offered a grand prize of $100,000 to the airship which shall make the best record over a prescribed course, marked by captive balloons, at a speed of not less than 20 miles an hour. Quite a large number of aeronauts have

KANSAS BUILDING.

arranged to compete, and it is hoped that some of them will be able to carry off the great prize.

There are other prizes for balloon races and contests of various kinds aggregating $50,000. It is probable that there will be five or six dirigible balloons, airships and aeroplanes in actual competition for the grand prize; and from 10 to 20 competitors in the free balloon contests. There was a total of over 80 entries on June 1. The interest in aeronautics has received tremendous impulse from the announcements of this concourse.

The prizes are offered for achievement only, leaving the widest range of methods open to the competition. The amusement attraction feature has been entirely ignored, and serious work only encouraged.

No great contest of this kind has ever been held—the nearest approach to it being the periodical balloon races held in France. This great aeronautic contest, if largely participated in and successfully conducted, will be another epoch-making event, having a tremendous effect upon the arts, both of peace and war.

PHYSICAL CULTURE.

The large building on the Athletic track, to be used for the physical culture exhibit, cost about $140,000   The main entrance is flanked by towers, from which flags will be displayed when games are in progress   The gymnasium, the largest room in the building, is 70 by 106 2 feet with ceiling 40 feet in height   A running track, 18 laps to the mile, on a gallery 13 feet above the main floor, is a feature of this room   There are locker rooms, shower bath rooms, bowling and handball alleys, in fact, all the features calculated to make it an ideal place for the actual practice of physical culture   Lectures of the World's Olympic Course and the Physical Training Conventions are held in the gymnasium

Exhibits.—Physical culture has received higher recognition at this Exposition than at any previous World's Fair   It has a place as a department in the general classification and ample space and liberal allotment of funds. $150,000 has been provided by the Exposition Company for the worthy exploitation of man's progress toward an ideal physical development and training   Never before in the history of the world has there been such an elaborate program of continuous athletic contests as has been arranged for this Exposition. The great Olympic games are to be held here, this being the third since their revival   A fine athletic field has been laid out on the University tract for displaying these contests as exhibits, and the largest **Stadium** and track ever built in America has been constructed, with a field large enough for equestrian polo, football, baseball and other outdoor sports

OLYMPIC GAMES.

By a decision of the International Olympic Committee all sports and competitions during the World's Fair are designated as Olympic events, with the exception of competitions for the championships of local associations   But one week—August 29 to September 3—has been set aside for the **Third Olympiad**, when the Olympic games proper are to be held   Teams are in the competition from England, Germany France, Ireland, Scotland and Australia the latter represented by four of its fastest track men

The program for the week is as follows

Aug 29 60 meter run throwing 16-lb hammer 400 meter run 2500 meter steeplechase, standing broad jump running high jump
   30 **MARATHON RACE,** 40 kilometers (about 25 miles)
   31 200 meter run, putting 16-lb shot lifting bar bell, standing high jump, international tug-of-war (trials) teams of five men each weight unlimited 40 meter hurdle race
Sept 1 800 meter run, throwing 56-lb weight for distance, 200 meter hurdle race, running broad jump, running hop, step and jump, tug-of-war (final), dumb-bell competition first section
   3 100 meter run throwing the discus, dumb-bell, second section, 1500 meter run, 110 meter hurdle pole vault for height, three standing jumps

International team race each country to start five men—distance four miles   The team scoring the highest number of points to win   Scoring to be 1 point for first, 2 points for second, etc

The classic Marathon race will be the great event of the week   Appropriate gold silver and bronze medals emblematic of the Olympic Championship, will be given to the winners in each event

WOMAN AT THE EXPOSITION.

The recognition accorded to woman in the plan and scope of the World's Fair is perhaps one of its most distinctive features

Woman's status in the affairs of the Exposition is traceable primarily to woman's own estimate of herself and her true position at this period of the world's advancement, and secondarily to man's recognition of this estimate.

Sec. 6 of the Special Act of Congress of March 3, 1901, which made the giving of the Exposition an assurity, provided that the National Commission of the Louisiana Purchase Exposition be "authorized to appoint a Board of Lady Managers of such number and to perform such duties as may be prescribed by said Commission, subject, however, to the approval of said Company. Said Board of Lady Managers may, in the discretion of said Commission and corporation, appoint one member of all committees authorized to award prizes for such exhibits as may have been produced in whole or in part by female labor." This was the recognition given to women in the Exposition by the National Government, voicing the wish of the beloved chieftain, President McKinley.

KENTUCKY BUILDING.

For the first time in the history of American expositions the World's Fair of 1904 is operated entirely upon a competitive basis, without regard for race, color or sex. It is argued that while it is unquestionably true that the really distinctive work of women as women in the highest and broadest sense can not be exhibited, it is also true that in every avenue of endeavor where a woman competes directly with a man, whether in art, education, industry or economics, the result of her labor is entitled to equal consideration with his. This is the basis of competition adopted by the Louisiana Purchase Exposition; therefore, among the gigantic palaces that make up the beautiful "Ivory City" of 1904 there is to be found no woman's building, the home of the Board of Lady Managers being used for purely administrative and social purposes.

While the participation of women in the Exposition extends with few exceptions to every department, for either in the way of clerical service, or by suggestion, assistance or actual exhibition, they have contributed in no small way to the success and welfare of the Exposition from its inciptency, the real "woman's part" is represented by the Board of Lady Managers, created by Act of Congress and appointed by the National Commission In so far as this is true, the Board of Lady Managers is national in character, and properly represents the women of the nation

The Board of Lady Managers has, since its appointment, endeavored to promote the interests of the Exposition in every line possible, and has accomplished not a little in the way of exploitation, both at home and abroad, and in assisting to secure State and National appropriations for furthering the work of the Exposition. Through its President, and with the assistance of the Department of State at Washington, the Board has issued invitations to the women of foreign countries asking their co-operation, assistance and presence to the end that the Fair may be a success from the woman's point of view.

While the Board of Lady Managers is authorized to exercise general supervisory control over all that pertains to woman's part of the Exposition, its highest prerogative is that granted by Congress in specifying that it should appoint one member of every jury of awards that is to judge the work in whole or in part the product of female labor This high privilege placed the Board in a position to give recognition in the fullest to the excellence of women in any particular line of endeavor and to set forth that recognition by choosing those who were fittest to serve upon the international jury of awards of the Louisiana Purchase Exposition

At no Exposition hitherto given have the social features been so strongly emphasized as at this Throughout the Exposition period it will be the pleasure and the privilege of the Board of Lady Managers to act as the hostesses of the nation. The building set apart for their use by the Exposition Company is one of the University group, being the southwest wing running back from the Hall of Congresses Here the Board of Lady Managers keep open house throughout the Exposition period, and are "at home" to women from all parts of the world A great banqueting hall, spacious drawing-rooms, handsome salons comfortable resting places and cozy tea-rooms find a place in the Board's suite, which will be open to the public during the usual Exposition hours, except at such times as the Board may be holding a social function, when the public must be excluded The Board also joins in the support of the model play grounds (See article on "Model Street ")

Statuary by Women —No enumeration of the work of women at the Fair would be complete without some reference to the part played by them in the decorative scheme of the Exposition Some of the most conspicuous pieces of statuary are by women

The fine "Victory" crowning the summit of Festival Hall is the handiwork of Miss Evelyn B Longman.

The entire interior decoration of the United States Government building is the work of Grace Lincoln Temple, of Washington, D C

"The Spirit of Missouri" crowning the dome of the Missouri building, is by Miss Carrie Wood, of St. Louis

Other prominent contributions of statuary by women are: "James Monroe," on the east approach of Art Hill, by Julia M Bracken, of Chicago, "James Madison," left approach to Cascade, by Miss Janet Scudder, Terre Haute, Ind , "George Rogers Clarke," on the west approach by Elsie Ward, of Denver On the Pagoda Cafes of the

LOUISIANA BUILDING (The Cabildo).

Grand Basin, two figures of "Victory" by Enid Yandell, of New York; also "Daniel Boone," at the approach to Art Hill the reclining figures over the broken pediment of the central door (Main Triumphal Arch) of the Liberal Arts building are by Edith B Stevens, New York, the east and north spandrels of the Machinery building by Melva Beatrice Wilson, New York

The manager of the Alaska exhibit is Mrs Mary E Hart, and women occupy many positions of responsibility and trust with the several state and territorial commissions

In the Palace of Fine Arts woman's work is apparent on every hand In the American section are three examples of the work of Cecelia Beaux, who has no superiors and few equals in the field of portrait painting Mrs Kenyon Cox takes rank with her gifted husband. Estelle Dickson, Margaret Fuller and Mary MacMonnies are all well known and are capably represented The portrait miniatures by Adele Winckler are among the finest examples of painting on ivory to be seen in the entire exhibit, where so much beautiful work by women is shown Mary Reid in the Canadian section, Virginia Demont-Breton in the French, Paula Monje and Clara Lobedau in the German and Lady Alma-Tadema and Henrietta Rae in the British sections are especially worthy of notice

MUSIC AT THE EXPOSITION.

The Bureau of Music has arranged elaborately for the entertainment of the visitors at the Exposition A goodly appropriation was granted Experience has proven that the general public is very much interested in band music, so the best bands in America, and some of the greatest foreign bands, have been engaged. Of the latter the Garde Republicaine band of Paris (by many considered the most remarkable band in the world) will be heard during the month of September The Mexican band of 63 pieces was present in August. The British Grenadier Guards Band (so dear to the hearts of the English people) comes for a six weeks' stay The Berlin Philharmonic Band, under the celebrated conductor, Von Blon, renders the great master works of the German composers Among the American bands are the world-renowned Sousa organization and the Boston, Innes, Sorrentino, Conterno, Weber, Creatore, Ellery, Haskell Indian, and other bands A St Louis band has a permanent engagement lasting throughout the Exposition There are two fine Philippine Bands and a Government Indian Band besides Government Military Bands render concerts daily at the Government building

There are six attractive band stands on the grounds and three bands are heard daily, concerts being given every afternoon and evening (See 'Band Stands" in article on "Classified Information")

An orchestra of 80 carefully selected players gives concerts at stated times during the season in Festival Hall, which is excellently adapted for the purpose Mr Alfred Ernst for nine years conductor of the St Louis Choral-Symphony Society, is director The programs are dignified without being too severe, and the price of admission is 25 cents Soloists of reputation are heard at some of the concerts When not used at Festival Hall the orchestra plays twice daily at one of The Pike concessions Two famous European conductors lead the orchestra at the concession concerts and the music to be heard will be of a bright and popular character Josef Hellmesberger, of

Vienna, conducted them until August 15, and Karl Komzak, also of Vienna, succeeded him remaining until the close of the Exposition

The largest organ in the world, installed in Festival Hall, is played upon daily by celebrated organists (See description under "Special Features of Interest ") A feature will be daily recitals by M Alexandre Guilmant of Paris, unquestionably the foremost living organist and one of the few really great composers for the organ Another celebrated organist who will play (November 8-9-10) is Edwin H Lemare, formerly of England, but recently appointed organist at the Carnegie Institute in Pittsburg Mr. Clarence Eddy, of New York whose reputation is international appears during the season Mr Charles Galloway, of St Louis, is the official organist The admission to all organ recitals is 10 cents

Among the organists who will perform on the great organ in Festival Hall are the following (dates subject to change)

J V Flagler Auburn, N Y, June 1, 2, H J Zehn Charlotte N C June 3 4 H H Hunt, Minneapolis June 6, 7, N H Allen, Hartford June 8, 9, H M Dunham Boston, June 10, 11 H M Wild Chicago, June 13 14, Mrs M C Fisher Rochester, June 15 16, R H Woodman, New York June 17, 18, G M Dethier, New York June 20, 21, H Parker New Haven June 22, 23, G W Andrews Oberlin, June 24 25, E M Bowman New York, June 27 28, W Middleschulte Chicago June 29 30 F J Reisberg New York July 1 2 N J Corey Detroit, July 4 5, G E Whiting Boston July 6 7 W X Steiner Pittsburg Pa July 8 9, G Smith New York July 11, 12, F P Tisk Kansas City July 13 14, W J Golph, Buffalo N Y, July 15, 16, J W Andrews New York July 18, 19, J O Shea Boston July 20, 21, J J Bishop Springfield Mass July 22 23, W S Sterling Cincinnati July 25 26 S N Penfield, New York, July 27, 28, H O Thunder, Philadelphia July 29 30, A J Epstein St Louis, August 1 2 A Raymond Boston August 3, 4, H Housclev Denver August 5 6, C S Howe New York August 8 9, S A Gibson New York, August 10, 11, H D Wilkins, Rochester August, 12 13 A Guilmant Paris (date open), W C Carl, New York September 26 27, F Dunkley New Orleans, September 28 29, E C Gale, New York September 30, October 1, J L Browne, Atlanta October 3 4, H N Shelley New York October 5 6, W Kaftenberger Buffalo October 7 8 F York Detroit October 10 11, W McFarlane New York, October 12 13 R K Miller, Philadelphia October 14, 15, E E Truette, Boston, October 17 18, F J Benedict, New York October 19 20, J A Pennington Scranton, October 21 22, A Ingham St Louis, October 24, 25 W H Donley Indianapolis, October 26 27 J F Wolle Bethlehem, Pa, October 28 29, W C Hammond, Holyoke Mass, October 31 November 1, Miss G Sans Souci, Minneapolis November 2, 3, A Dunham Chicago November 4 5, R H Peters Spartansburg S C November 7 L H Lemare Pittsburg November 8 9 10 G H Chadwick Chicago November 11 12, E Kreiser Kansas City, November 14, 15, L L Renwick Ann Arbor, November 16 17, S Salter New York, November 18 19 L Holloway Baltimore November 21, 22, H B Day New York November 23 24, F C Chace Albion Mich, November 25 26 A Scott-Brook, Los Angeles November 28 29 C Galloway St Louis, November 30

Some of the best Choral Societies in the land give concerts of standard and modern works Choral contests for large prizes took place the second week of July and will be followed by the Male Chorus contests In September, band contests take place The aggregate amount of the prizes offered for the latter is $30 000

The school children will be heard in massed concerts in the Stadium, as well as in Festival Hall

Much special music in reference to National and State occasions will be rendered, and American composers works will be heard frequently Occasional recitals will be heard in the small Recital Hall (situated in one of the wings of Festival Hall)

THE MILITARY.

Every day of the entire seven months that the Exposition is open is taken up by some State, or by some military or fraternal organization, or other body, as a special day of celebration. Nearly every date has some special feature assigned it, and many have several.

There are encamped at the grounds at different times various regular troops, the cadets from the United States Military Academy at West Point, and National Guard organizations from a number of States. Cadets from many military schools, accompanied by their tutors, are also availing themselves of the invitation to camp at the big Fair.

The West Point cadets were at the Fair Grounds from May 30 to June 9.

Under the direction of their officers, the National Guard of the

MINNESOTA BUILDING.

various States will, while encamped at the Fair, study the Government war exhibits, the gradual change of equipment since the early days of the Republic, and other interesting features.

Seven barracks have been built, each capable of accommodating 256 men. The barracks are located just south of the Aeronautic Concourse, east of the Physical Culture grounds.

The parade grounds adjoin the barracks, and in addition we have the Grand Plaza of St. Louis, facing Cascade Hill, which is used for the evolutions and drills of uniformed organizations and for great open air gatherings too large and too popular to be held within walls.

The Exposition also supplies within its gates a camp ground area, covered with beautiful blue grass sod. These grounds are located south of the big University Dormitory and are easily accessible by the Intramural.

CLASSIFIED EXPOSITION INFORMATION.

Admission Fee to Fair Grounds: Adults, 50 cents; Children under 12 years, 25 cents; under 5, free. Season tickets, good for 184 admissions, are sold for $25. Season tickets good for 50 admissions were sold for $12.50, later for $15. Monthly tickets, 15 admissions, may be had for $5. The photograph of the purchaser is printed on the cover of most of the coupon tickets, which are non-transferable.

Automobilists at Fair.—The National Automobile Association reached St. Louis on the evening of Wednesday, August 10, and 63 chauffeurs took part in the celebration, riding through the Exposition grounds on their machines. The start of the Association was made from New York City, and the trip to St. Louis was via Chicago. A grand automobile parade, participated in by over 250 machines, was a feature of Automobile Day, August 12.

Baggage.—Baggage may be checked from any house back to destination. Orders for baggage calls must be left with the St. Louis

MISSISSIPPI BUILDING.

Transfer Company (baggage department), or with any railroad ticket office at least 24 hours before the baggage is to be called for. Railway tickets to the point to which the baggage is to be checked must be shown to the baggageman at the house or hotel. Before trains reach the city, agents of the Transfer Company pass through, checking trunks and providing bus or carriage transportation to any part of the city. Only hand baggage may be carried on street cars. The Transfer Company have a baggage office at 506 Chestnut, and one in the general baggage room at Union Station. The charges range from 35 cents to $1.00 for each piece of baggage checked, depending on the distance from Union Station.

Band Stands.—Bands play at stated times in six band stands located at various points on the Exposition grounds. At least two programs are rendered daily at each stand, a different band appearing on each occasion. The stands are located as follows: Two at the north end of the Plaza of St. Louis; one each at south end of Plaza of Orleans; in front of the U. S. Government building; at the east end of Garden, between Palaces of Machinery and Transportation, at the west end of Garden between Palaces of Machinery and Transportation, at the west court. Cascade Gardens. Concerts are also given at frequent intervals on the Plateau of States in front of the Administration building and in the Philippine reservation, by the Philippine Scout and Constabulary Bands. (See articles on "Philippine Encampment" and "Music at the Exposition".) The band at the Government Indian School is extremely good. A U S Military Band gives daily concerts at the Government building.

Bank at Grounds—The Bankers' World's Fair National Bank of St Louis occupies a building on Plaza of St. Louis, 84 by 54 feet and two stories high. This institution is a joint enterprise of seventeen of the leading bank and trust companies of St Louis and transacts the World's Fair grounds business for all of them. It is capitalized at $200,000, but the total capital and resources of the institution's backing foots up several hundred millions, making it probably the most powerful financial concern in America. The same institutions interested in the bank also conduct a trust and safe deposit company with it in the same building.

Bazaar Charges—Cash registers are used in the bazaars to register each purchase and to prevent overcharges.

Board and Lodging Information—The World's Fair has connected with it what is known as the "Free Information Service of the Louisiana Purchase Exposition." This bureau has an office in the Laclede building, Fourth and Olive streets. Here is kept a complete list of hotels boarding and rooming houses and private residences that will take care of visitors during the Exposition period.

Boats and Gondolas—Seats in electric launches may be secured at the various landings. 25 cents per person, gondolas 50 cents per person.

Cameras and Kodaks—Tripod cameras or those taking pictures larger than 4 by 5 inches are prohibited, kodaks taking 4 by 5 pictures or less are allowed.

Checking Booths—Bundles may be checked for a small fee at a number of check rooms established for the purpose at the several entrances.

Checking Babies—Babies, for a small fee may be checked at the Model Play-grounds, Model City.

Clothing—During the months of May and June, September and October, light overcoats and wraps are desirable for cool days and evenings. During July and August usual summer attire is seasonable. For November the use of slightly heavier outer garments is suggested.

Colors—The official colors of the Exposition are emblematic of the three Governments associated in the history of the Louisiana Purchase—United States of America, France and Spain. The official flag shows a field of blue with fleur de lis and 14 stars in white, and three broad stripes red white and yellow. The 14 stars signify the States carved from the Louisiana territory.

Concession tickets are used for admission to all attractions on The Pike. The tickets are supplied in rolls by the Concessions department of the Exposition and sold the price being printed on each in large letters.

Distillery in operation, in which the production of spirituous liquors is carried on for public inspection, is located south of the Palace of Forestry, Fish and Game. A special United States Government permit has been taken out for its operation, and the warehouses adjoining have been made Government bonded warehouses for the handling of the product.

Eating Places.—(See "Restaurants.")

Emblem.—The fleur de lis is the official emblem of the Exposition.

Exposition Offices.—The general officers of the Exposition Company have their offices in the Administration building, but the chief of each exhibit department has his office in the palace in which the displays in his particular department are made. Commissioners of

MONTANA BUILDING.

States and Foreign Governments maintain offices in their respective pavilions.

Express Companies.—Except the Pacific, all the express companies have an office on the Model Street and deliver packages on the ground free. The Pacific express office is in the Wabash depot at Lindell Entrance. (See article on Express Companies in "Facts About St. Louis.")

Fire Protection.—A complete system of fire protection and prevention is installed on the grounds at a cost to the Exposition of over $650,000. About 36 miles of pipe for high pressure fire protection system have been installed, covering the Exposition grounds and main exhibit buildings. Five engine houses have been constructed and equipped. The interior of the exhibit buildings is protected by hydrants spaced 150 feet apart, each with hose attached. In high towels and under elevated portions of floor of Art buildings, sprinkler systems have been installed. Chemical fire extinguishers are placed at convenient points about each building There are call boxes, telegraph signals, etc , and the firemen and Jefferson Guards are thoroughly trained for the prevention of fire

Garbage Plant.—A garbage crematory has been erected northwest of the Philippine site, where combustible debris and garbage are taken care of, the moist garbage is deposited in cans at the buildings and is removed at night, combustible street sweepings are also taken to the garbage plant, being cared for in sacks made especially for this purpose Streets are swept at night and all except combustible material is hauled away to dumps in the western portion of the grounds

Inside the exhibit palaces the department chiefs have a system of janitor service

Guides —(See "Roller Chairs ")

Historic Buildings —A number of historic buildings and spots are reproduced at the Exposition, among them are House in which Daniel Webster was born, at Concord, N H , reproduced by New Hampshire as its State building; the old Constitution House at Windsor, Vt , in which the first Constitution of Vermont was adopted, reproduced by the State as its building, Robert Burns' Cottage, reproduced at the corner of Administration Av and Skinker Road (University Bl), just east of the Holland pavilion and opposite the British pavilion; General Grant's Cabin, moved from Old Orchard and rebuilt from original material, near Palace of Fine Arts, Beauvoir, Jefferson Davis' Mansion, reproduced by Mississippi as State headquarters, Washington's Headquarters at Morristown during Revolutionary War, reproduced by New Jersey as the State building, Andrew Jackson's Hermitage, reproduced as Tennessee's State building, Monticello, Thomas Jefferson's home, reproduced as Virginia's State building, The Cabildo, where the formal transfer of the Louisiana territory occurred, reproduced by the State of Louisiana; La Rabida, the old mission building at Santa Barbara, reproduced by the State of California for its building, Roosevelt's Cabin displayed by North Dakota in the Palace of Agriculture

Intramural Road.—Fare for trip or between stations, 10 cents.

Jefferson Guard —On February 13, 1902, Lieutenant-Colonel E A Godwin, Ninth Cavalry, United States Army, was designated by the War Department to organize and discipline the Jefferson Guard, to be formed for use at the Louisiana Purchase Exposition In February, 1904, Colonel Godwin was, at his own request, relieved from duty with the Louisiana Purchase Exposition and was replaced by Lieutenant-Colonel Henry P. Kingsbury, of the Eighth Cavalry, who is at present Commandant

The strength of the Guard April 1, 1904, was 300 men When the organization is complete and the Fair in full progress there will be somewhere between 600 and 1 000 men The Guards are carefully selected men, must be between the ages of 21 and 40 at least 5 feet 8 inches in height, between 145 and 180 pounds in weight, according to height, and of good figure and bearing, and must be physically sound The pay is $50 per month, and sleeping quarters The men board themselves

Jinrikshas —75 cents an hour, 40 cents half hour

Lagoons have an area of 750,000 square feet and contain 20 000,000 gallons of water, the depth varying from 3½ feet to 5 feet. Electric launches and gondolas afford a continuous trip of 1½ miles. The lagoons are provided with six feed pipes from water mains of such capacity that the entire lake can be filled in 40 hours. Filter plant at southwest corner of Liberal Arts building is designed to supply the loss from seepage and evaporation and will be operated continuously during the life of the Fair.

Launches and Barges.—(See "Boats.")

Life Saving Service.—(See "Treasury Department" in article on "Government Building and Exhibits.")

Lost Children.—Lost children should be turned over to the Jefferson Guards. The Board of Lady Managers have provided a room at

NEVADA BUILDING.

the Model Playgrounds, Model Street, where these little ones will be taken care of until called for.

Lost property is cared for by the Jefferson Guards and may be recovered by the loser on proper identification.

Lumber Used.—In the construction of the Exposition there were used over 132,500,000 feet of lumber. In boards 12 inches wide and 1 inch thick this would equal 25,350 miles, or more than enough to girdle the entire world.

Lunch boxes may be brought to the Exposition, and the free use of certain of the benches placed around the grounds by the Exposition Company is permitted for luncheon purposes. Supplies may be purchased by luncheon parties at near-by restaurants and carried to these seats.

Medical Assistance.—An emergency hospital for the care of visitors requiring it located in the Model Street, is equipped with a full corps of physicians, nurses attendants and all the latest appliances known to medical science The staff, consisting of 9 surgeons, 9 orderlies, 9 stretcher bearers 10 trained nurses and 5 ambulances, is in charge of Dr L. H Laidley, Medical Director of the Exposition A signal system is in operation all over the grounds whereby ambulances may be summoned In case of sickness apply to one of the Jefferson Guards who will summon an ambulance There is no charge for this service

Olympic Games.—These athletic contests are held every four years and are a revival of the celebrated contests of ancient Greece. Eight years ago they were held at Athens, Greece, and four years ago at Paris, France They are international in character

Parcels and Packages.—(See "Checking Booths')

Post Offices.—A perfectly equipped U S Post Office, known as the 'Exposition Post Office," is in the U S Government building, where it is placed by the U S Post Office department as a model From this branch 14 carriers make deliveries to all buildings, booths and concessions

Press Pavilion, a permanent building located near the Lindell Entrance, in architecture is a mingling of the public building style and the homestead type of the early days of the Louisiana territory This was the first building on the World's Fair grounds to be completed It is intended as a club house for visiting newspaper men.

Reduced Railroad Rates.—The various passenger associations of the United States have made special rates to the St Louis World's Fair During the entire period of the Exposition stop-over privileges at St Louis of ten days are allowed on all through one-way and round-trip tickets to points beyond St Louis upon payment of a fee of $1 Beginning April 25 and continuing during the Exposition period with a final return limit of December 15, a round-trip rate was made by all lines of 80 per cent double the one-way fare Excursion tickets good for 60 days are sold by all lines at a round-trip rate of one and one-third the regular fare one way, a minimum of $5 being made by the Southwestern lines Excursion tickets limited to ten days from most points and to 15 days from points far removed from St Louis, are sold at the one-fare rate, plus $2

Restaurants.—Eating places installed on the Exposition grounds number about 125 Of these, about 75 are restaurants and the remainder, 50, are lunch counters There is great variety as to prices and service The restaurants have an entire capacity of seating 30,000 people at the same time, and 100,000 people may be fed three times daily without overtaxing The most important restaurants are: **On the Pike,** from the east German Tyrolean Alps, Parliament House, (Irish Village), Streets of Seville Hagenbeck Mysterious Asia, Moorish Palace Fair Japan, Hereafter, Paris Ancient Rome, Indian Congress Old St Louis, Palais du Costume, Siberian Railway, Cairo, Chinese Village, Constantinople Esquimaux Village, Magic Whirlpool, Cliff Dwellers Old Plantation, Water Chutes Scenic Railway, Naval Exhibit, Hale's Fire Fighters **East side of grounds:** Vienna Cafe, east end Model Street, Rice Kitchen Model Street American Inn, Model Street, Government east of Model Street northeast of Liberal Arts Marine Corps, south of Marine Corps camp, Ionic near Parade Entrance. **West side of grounds:** Administration, west of Brazil; Military, west of Administration building; Japanese Tea House, east of Observation Wheel; Falstaff, north of Observation Wheel; Ceylon Tea, Ceylon pavilion; India pavilion; Blatz, west of Station 8; Crystal Cafe, north of Jerusalem; Jerusalem concession; Model Poultry, opposite Station 9; Danish, near Philippine bridge; Swedish, south of Observation Wheel; Guatemala; Morocco, west of Jerusalem; Temple Inn, north of Temple of Fraternity. **Art Hill:** Mrs. Rorer, east pavilion; Faust, west pavilion; German, next Das Deutsche Haus; Hoo-Hoo Cafe, south of German pavilion. **South side of grounds:** Bird Cage Cafe, south of Government building; Nebraska, southwest of New York building; Coal Mine, in Anthracite Mining exhibit; Park View, south of Metal pavilion; Vermont State building; Inside Inn hotel, State Buildings Entrance; Grant's Log Cabin, southeast Fine Arts building; Palm Cottage, opposite Station 11; Southern Home, opposite

NEW JERSEY BUILDING.

Station 12. **In exhibit palaces:** Southwest entrance, Agriculture; Ralston exhibit, Agriculture; German exhibit, Agriculture; Block 27, Agriculture; Block 140, Agriculture; Manufactures building; Horticulture building; Live Stock Plateau. **Intramural Stations:** Lunch stands on Nos. 1, 2, 3, 6, 8, 9, 14, 17.

River Trips.—During the summer months popular day and night excursions are conducted by the steamboat companies operating on the Mississippi, giving visitors opportunity to view the harbor and the many points of interest above and below the city. Price 25 cents and 50 cents for the round trip. More extended trips are made at stated intervals, and packet lines carry passengers to Upper Mississippi river points on fixed sailing days. Due announcements are made in the daily newspapers.

Roads at the Fair.—A total area of 5,800,000 square feet has been paved with ballast, gravel, macadam, asphalt and brick This is equal to about 75 miles of walk 25 feet wide

Roller chairs may be engaged with or without guides The charge for uniformed guide and chair is 60 cents an hour, guide without chair, 35 cents an hour Chairs without guides may be secured on depositing $5 as security for each chair. Chairs may be engaged by 'phone to meet visitors at designated places without extra charge.

Sanitation of the Exposition is on a scientific basis Specially constructed sewers were installed by the Exposition Company as the first work of preparation for the site These discharge by gravity into two wells in the eastern end of the grounds, near the Palace of Mines and Metallurgy, from which sewage is pumped into the city sewer mains a distance of 3,650 feet through a 27-inch cast-iron main. Four electrically-driven centrifugal pumps, of 18,000,000 gallons capacity, have been installed for this service

Sea-Coast Defense Drills.—(See "War Department" in article on "Government Building and Exhibits.")

Smoking.—Smoking is permitted anywhere on the grounds, but not in the exhibit palaces

Souvenir Gold Coins.—The only commemorative or souvenir coin of the Exposition is a gold dollar, issued under a special Act of Congress and known as the Louisiana dollar. This coin is of two types, one bearing the head of Thomas Jefferson, President in 1803; the other being an excellent profile of the late William McKinley The product has been pronounced by numismatists the finest example of die engraving and metal stamping extant The issue is limited to 125,000 of each type Price $3 00 each, and none will be sold for less This coin is furnished in various forms of jewelry without additional charge

Souvenir Stamps —Louisiana Purchase souvenir postage stamps were placed on sale by the U S Government, and their sale will be continued through the Exposition period The total issue required, it is estimated, will considerably exceed one billion The stamps are as follows 1-cent, green, with portrait of Robert R Livingston, United States Minister to France who conducted the Louisiana purchase negotiations. 2-cent, red, portrait of Thomas Jefferson, President of the United States at the time of the purchase, 3-cent, purple, portrait of James Monroe, special ambassador to France, who, with Livingston, closed the negotiations for the purchase, 5 cent, blue, portrait of William McKinley, who, as President, approved the act of Congress officially connecting the United States with the Exposition, and 10-cent, brown, bearing a United States map showing the territory of the purchase

Stadium seating capacity is 27,000

Staff —The material known as staff, which enters so largely into the construction of an exposition, is made of a composition of plaster of paris and hemp fibre. It forms the covering of most of the buildings, and the statuary scrolls, allegorical groups and other pieces of sculpture are made of it Over the sculptor's model of clay a shell is built, and a composition of gelatine or glue is poured into the space between This forms a reverse mold, or matrix, and into it the staff decoration is cast It may be handled almost like lumber, sawed, nailed and repaired, and is quite durable Without staff, which is cheap and quickly made, the building of such temporary palaces and statuary would be impracticable.

States in Louisiana Purchase.—The following States and Territories were formed from the domain acquired by the Louisiana purchase: Louisiana, Arkansas, Missouri, Oklahoma, Indian Territory, Kansas, Colorado, Nebraska, Iowa, Minnesota, North Dakota, South Dakota, Wyoming and Montana—14 in all. The population of the territory was, exclusive of Indians, between 80,000 and 100,000. It is now about 15,000,000. The territory acquired by the Louisiana purchase is greater than the combined area of France, Germany, England, Scotland, Ireland, Wales, the Netherlands, Belgium, Italy and Spain. The United States paid for this territory $15,000,000 one hundred years ago.

NEW YORK BUILDING.

Telegraph Stations.—Both systems of telegraph, W. U. and Postal, have stations at convenient points throughout the grounds. The main station for each system is located in the Palace of Electricity, near the main door at the center of the north front, where the manager is stationed. Sub-stations are located as follows: Palaces of Mines and Metallurgy, Transportation, Manufactures, Varied Industries, Machinery and Agriculture, Administration building, New York State building, and in the Inside Inn. There is a sub-station also on The Pike. Messages will be received and delivered to addresses on the Exposition grounds at regular city rates.

Telephones.—Telephone pay stations of the Bell and Kinloch systems are located at convenient places on the grounds and in all the exhibit palaces. Each company has a model exchange in Palace of Electricity.

Thirty Million Plants.—In the embellishment of the World's Fair landscape features thirty million flowering and budding plants have been employed.

Ticket Offices are located in the Transportation building, east wing, where tickets can be purchased over any railroad, and sleeping car berths can be secured. This is also a joint validating office. Another **validating office** is situated just outside the grounds near the main entrance.

Toilet rooms are installed in each exhibit palace and in the smaller buildings. Some of these are free and at others a small fee is charged. **Outside toilet rooms** are situated near the following: Press building; northeast corner of Palace of Varied Industries; east wing of Art Palace; Athletic Field grandstand; U. S. Government Bird Cage;

OKLAHOMA BUILDING.

southwest of Art Palace; south side of The Pike, just north of Palace of Transportation; also water closets and toilet conveniences have been supplied in a number of Intramural stations. (For complete list see "Index to Location" on map of the grounds.) Plumbing is looked after by special inspectors who regularly **disinfect all fixtures.**

Transportation Within the Grounds.—To see the Exposition every possible facility for the economy of the visitor's time and the saving of his strength is provided. Boats will traverse the mile or more of lagoons which surround the Electricity and Education Palaces and an Intramural Railway reaches every part of the grounds. Rolling chairs and jinrikshas may be secured for trips through the buildings and elsewhere. Automobiles also traverse the grounds.

U. S. Marine Corps, known as "sea soldiers," are encamped east of the Model City. Two hundred marines give daily exhibitions on the Plaza.

Vehicles—Vehicles of all kinds must enter by the State Buildings Entrance and travel over a prescribed course.

Windows—In the windows of the Palace of Agriculture there are 147,250 panes of glass 18 by 25 inches. In the Belgian National building there are no windows.

Waiter's checks at restaurants are stamped by agents of the concessions department of the Exposition and the amount of the bill appears in plain figures.

SPECIAL DAYS AND CONVENTIONS.

SEPTEMBER

1	Tennessee
	Indiana
1- 2	Jewelers and Silversmiths
1- 3	Society for Promotion of Engineering Education
1-15	National Guard of California Co. D 7th Infantry
2	Fraternal Aid Association
3	Opticians
	Sons and Daughters of Justice
3- 4	International Dental Congress
4-10	Modern Woodmen of America
5	Oklahoma City
5- 9	Modern Woodmen of America Foresters Teams
5-10	International Interparliamentary Congress
6	Oklahoma
	Woodmen's Modern Protective Association
6- 8	National Association of Master Plumbers
7	United National Association of Post Office Clerks
	Alumni Wells College
	Royal Neighbors
	Brigham Family Reunion
8	Modern Woodmen of America
9	California—Anniversary of Admission into Union
	House of Hoo-Hoo
	Odd Fellows Day
9-13	American Roentgen Ray Society
10	Spanish War Veterans
	Order of Mutual Protection
10-17	Trans-Mississippi Commercial Congress
12	Maryland—Anniversary of Battle of North Point
	International Stewards
12-14	Interparliamentary Conference
12-17	Massachusetts Volunteer Militia
	Third International Congress on Electricity
13	Catholic Knights of America
13-15	American Association of Obstetricians and Gynecologists
13-17	American Electro-Therapeutic Association
13-18	National Association of Master Bakers
14	Louisiana
	Woodmen of the World
	Woodmen's Circle
14-16	Acetylene Gas Congress
15	**ST. LOUIS DAY**
	Farmers
	German Catholics' Central Verein
	The Home Circle
	National Association of Laundrymen
15-16	Southern Live Stock Association
15-17	American Neurological Association
16	Mexico—Anniversary of Independence
	Germanic Congress
	Modern Maccabees

— 155 —

OHIO BUILDING.

ATHLETIC EVENTS

AUGUST

SEPTEMBER

CLASSIFICATION OF EXHIBIT DEPARTMENTS.

General Departments—There are fifteen General Departments of the Exposition, as follows (with subdivisions)

A Education—Elementary, Secondary, Higher, Special Education in Fine Arts, Special Education in Agriculture, Special Education in Commerce and Industry, Education of Detectives, Special Forms of Education, textbooks, school furniture and appliances

B Art—Paintings and Drawings, Engravings and Lithographs, Sculpture, Architecture, Art Workmanship

C Liberal Arts—Typography, Photography, Books and Publications, Maps and Apparatus for Geography, Cosmography, Topography, Instruments of Precision, Philosophical Apparatus, Coins and Models, Medicine and Surgery, Musical Instruments, Theatrical Appliances and Equipment, Chemical and Pharmaceutical Arts, Manufacture of Paper, Civil and Military Engineering, Models, Plans and Designs for Public Works, Architectural Engineering

D Manufactures—Stationery, Cutlery, Silversmiths and Goldsmiths Wares, Jewelry, Clock and Watchmaking, Production in Marble, Bronze, Cast Iron and Wrought Iron, Brushes, Fine Leather Articles, Fancy Articles and Basket Work, Articles for Traveling and Camping, India Rubber and Gutta Percha Industries, Toys, Decorative and Fixed Furniture for Buildings and Dwellings, Office and Household Furniture, Stained Glass, Mortuary Monuments and Undertakers' Furnishings, Hardware, Paper Hanging, Carpets, Tapestries and Fabrics for Upholstering, Upholsterers' Decorations, Ceramics, Plumbing and Sanitary Materials, Glass and Crystal Apparatus and Processes for Heating and Ventilation, Apparatus and Methods (not Electrical) for Lighting, Textile Materials and Processes for Spinning and Rope-making, Equipment and Processes Used in the Manufacture of Textile Fabrics, those used in Bleaching, Dyeing, Printing and Finishing Textiles, those used in Sewing and Making Wearing Apparel, Threads and Fabrics of Cotton, Threads and Fabrics of Flax, Hemp, etc, Cordage, Yarns and Fabrics of Wool, Silk and Fabrics of Silk, Laces, Embroidery and Trimmings, Industries producing Wearing Apparel for Men, Women and Children, Leather, Boots and Shoes, Furs and Skins For Clothing, Various Industries connected with Clothing

E   Machinery—Steam Engines, Various Motors, General Machinery; Machine Tools, Arsenal Tools

F   Electricity—Machines for Generating and Using Electricity, Electro-Chemistry, Electric Lighting, Telegraphy and Telephony; Various Applications of Electricity

G   Transportation.—Carriages and Wheelwright's Work, Automobiles and Cycles, Saddlery and Harness, Railways, Yards Stations, Freight Houses, Terminal Facilities of all kinds, Material and Equipment used in the Mercantile Marine, Material and Equipment of Naval Service, Naval Warfare, Aerial Navigation

H   Agriculture—Farm Equipment, Methods of Improving Lands, Agricultural Implements and Farm Machinery Fertilizers, Tobacco, Appliances and Methods Used in Agricultural Industries, Theory of Agriculture, Agricultural Statistics, Vegetable Food Products, Agricultural Seeds, Animal Food Products, Farinaceous Products and their Derivations, Bread and Pastry, Preserved Meat, Fish, Vegetables and Fruit, Sugar and Confectionery—Condiments and Relishes, Waters, Wines and Brandies, Syrups and Liquors—Distilled Spirits—Commercial Alcohols, Fermented Beverages, Inedible Agricultural Products, Insects and their Products—Plant Diseases

I   Live Stock—Horses and Mules, Cattle, Sheep, Goats, etc.; Swine, Dogs, Cats, Ferrets, etc., Poultry and Birds

J   Horticulture—Appliances and Methods of Pomology Floriculture and Arboriculture Appliances and Methods of Viticulture, Pomology, Trees, Shrubs, Ornamental Plants and Flowers Plants of the Conservatory, Seeds and Plants for Gardens and Nurseries, Arboriculture and Fruit Culture.

K   Forestry—Appliances and Processes used in Forestry, Products of the Cultivation of Forests and Forest Industries, Appliances for Gathering Wild Crops and Products Obtained

L   Mines and Metallurgy—Working of Mines Ore Beds and Stone Quarries, Minerals and Stones and their Utilization, Mine Models, Maps, Photographs, Metallurgy Literature of Mining Metallurgy etc

M   Fish and Game—Hunting Equipment, Products of Hunting, Fishing Equipment and Products, Products or Fisheries, Fish Culture

N   Anthropology—Literature, Somatology, Ethnology, Ethnography

O   Social Economy—Study and Investigation of Social and Economic Conditions, Economic Resources and Organizations, State Regulation of Industry and Labor, Organization of Industrial Workers, Methods of Industrial Remuneration Co-operative Institutions Provident Institutions, Housing of the Working Classes, the Liquor Question, General Betterment Movements Charities and Corrections, Public Health, Municipal Improvement

P   Physical Culture—Training of the Child and Adult—Theory and Practice, Games and Sports for Children and Adults, Equipment for Games and Sports

---

ORGANIZATION OF THE EXPOSITION.

DAVID R FRANCIS, President of the Louisiana Purchase Exposition Company

THOMAS H CARTER, President of the United States National Commission

WALTER B STEVENS Secretary of the Louisiana Purchase Exposition Company and Director of Exploitation

FREDERICK J V SKIFF Director of Exhibits

ISAAC S TAYLOR Director of Works

NORRIS B GREGG Director of Concessions and Admissions

LOUISIANA PURCHASE EXPOSITION OFFICERS

PRESIDENT—David R Francis

VICE-PRESIDENTS—First Corwin H Spencer Second, Samual M Kennard, Third Daniel M Houser, Fourth Cyrus P Walbridge, Fifth Seth W Cobb Sixth Charles H Huttig Seventh August Gehner, Eighth, Pierre Chouteau

TREASURER—William H Thompson

GENERAL COUNSEL—Franklin Ferris

PENNSYLVANIA BUILDING.

EXECUTIVE DIVISIONS

Exhibits Director, Frederick J. V. Skiff, Assistant to the Director, Edmund S. Hoch Chiefs—Education. Howard J. Rogers Art. Halsey C. Ives, Charles M. Kurtz, Assistant Chief Liberal Arts. John A. Ockerson Manufactures Milan H. Hulbert Machinery· Thomas M. Moore Electricity W. E. Goldsborough Transportation Willard A. Smith, A. C. Baker Assistant Chief Agriculture Fredric W. Taylor Horticulture. Fredric W. Taylor Forestry Tarleton H. Bean Mines and Metallurgy J. A. Holmes Fish and Game Tarleton H. Bean Anthropology W. J. McGee Social Economy. Howard J. Rogers Physical Culture James E. Sullivan Live Stock Chas. F. Mills, successor to F. D. Coburn Director of Congresses. Howard J. Rogers Chief of Bureau of Music George D. Markham

Exploitation Director, Walter B. Stevens Foreign. Chairman, Adolphus Busch Secretary Russell C. Stanhope Commissioners—Asia· John Barlett Europe Thomas W. Cridler Italy. Vittorio Zeggio Argentine Republic, Chili, Uruguay Paraguay and Bolivia Jose de Olivares Brazil and Portugal John Taylor Lewis Peru, Ecuador, Colombia and Venezuela· Ernest H. Wands Cuba· Charles M. Pepper Central American Countries John Rice Chandler India. Palmer L. Bowen South Africa, Australia and New Zealand C. A. Green Sweden and Norway Charles W. Kohlsaat Trinidad and Windward Islands G. W. Fishback Resident Representative in London George F. Parker Resident Representative in Berlin. Joseph Bruckel Foreign Press Commissioner Walter Williams Domestic· Chairman, Legislation D. M. Houser Chairman States and Territories, C. H. Huttig, Chief Charles M. Reeves Press and Publicity. General Press, Mark Bennitt, Local Press, W. A. Kelsoe, Publicity Edward Hooker Committee on Ceremonies Secretary, Allan V. Cockrell Committee on Reception and Entertainment Secretary Ricardo Diaz Albertini

Concessions and Admissions Director Norris B. Gregg, Chiefs—Concessions Jno. A. Wakefield Admissions E. Norton White, Press Representative for Pike· T. R. McMechin

Works Director Isaac S. Taylor Chiefs Design E. L. Masqueray, Sculpture Karl T. F. Bitter Mural Decoration Louis J. Millet, Landscape Architect George E. Kessler, Building Engineer, Philip J. Markmann, Electrical and Mechanical Engineer E. B. Ellicott,** Consulting Civil Engineer R. H. Phillips, Draughtsman, W. H. H. Weatherwax Advisory Committee of Sculptors J. Q. A. Ward Augustus St Gaudens, Daniel C French

Transportation Director John Scullin, General Manager C. L. Hilleary, Superintendent of Terminals, W. S. Carson, Superintendent of Intramural Railway Thos. W. Murph

Died · · · Vacancy not yet filled
Resigned

Miscellaneous Auditor Fred Gabel Traffic Manager C L Haleary, Medical Director Leonidas H Laidley M D, Commandant of Jefferson Guard Lt-Col Henry P Kingsbury 5th U S Cavalry Custodian of Buildings and Assistant to Secretary of Exposition Company J Bissell Ware

UNITED STATES COMMISSIONERS

National Commission (appointed by the President of the United States to represent U S Government) Hon Thomas H Carter Montana Chairman, Hon Martin H Glynn New York Vice-Chairman Hon J M Thurston Nebraska Hon Wm Lindsay Kentucky, Hon George W McBride, Oregon Hon John F Miller, Indiana Hon F A Betts Connecticut, Hon P D Scott Arkansas, Hon J M Allen Mississippi, Laurence H Grahame New York Secretary vice Joseph Flory, resigned

BOARD OF LADY MANAGERS
(Appointed by the United States Commissioners)

President Mrs Daniel Manning Washington D C Vice-Presidents 1st Mrs Edward L Buchwalter Springfield O 2d Mrs Finis P Ernest Denver, Colo 3d Mrs Helen Boice-Hunsiker Philadelphia Pa 4th Miss Anna L Dawes Pittsfield Mass 5th Mrs Lelle L Everest Atchison Kan, 6th Mrs M H de Young San Francisco Cal, 7th, Mrs Finnie L Porter, Atlanta Ga Miss Lavina H Egan Mrs William H Coleman Fresnoley, Miss Helen M Gould New York City, Mrs John M Holcombe Hartford Conn Mrs Frederick M Hanger Little Rock Ark Mrs W E Andrews Washington, D C, Mrs Richard W Knott, Louisville Ky, Mrs Margaret P Daly Anaconda Mont Mrs Louis D Frost Winona Mont, Mrs Mary Phelps Montgomery Portland Ore Mrs John Miller Horton Buffalo N Y, Mrs A L von Maxhoff New York City Mrs James Edmund Sullivan Providence R I Mrs Annie McLean Moores, Mt Pleasant Tex, Miss Etta L Carter, Clerical Secretary

U S GOVERNMENT BOARD

Government Board in Charge of U S Government Exhibit Wallace H Hills Treasury Department, Chairman vice J H Brigham (deceased), **Department of Justice**, Col Cecil Clay, **Labor Department**, G W W Hanger, **Post Office Department**, J B Brownlow **Fish Commissioner** Prof W de C Ravenel, **Interior Department**, Edward M Dawson **Bureau of American Republics**, William C Fox, **State Department**, William H Michael **Navy Department**, B F Peters **War Department**, J C Scofield **Smithsonian Institution**, Dr F W True W V Cox, Secretary, William M Geddes Disbursing Officer

---

COMMISSIONERS TO THE EXPOSITION.

EXECUTIVE OFFICERS ACCREDITED BY THEIR RESPECTIVE GOVERNMENTS TO THE EXPOSITION

FOREIGN COUNTRIES

Argentine—Dr Jose V Fernandez, Comm-Gen Argentine Pavilion, World's Fair Grounds

Austria—Chevalier Adalbert von Stibral Comm-Gen 3516 Morgan St Tel (Bell) Lindell 894A

Representing the Commercial Commission—Charles M Rosenthal Ex Comm, Max Pollitzer Private Secretary, 5671 Clemens Av Tel (Bell) Forest 1849

Belgium—Alfred Simonis Chairman of Commission Jules Carlier Comm-Gen, C Spruyt, Secretary, Washington Hotel Tel (Bell) Forest 1360, also The Belgian Pavilion

Brazil—Col F M de Souza Aguiar, Comm-Gen, Major J daCunha Pires Secretary, 427 Lake Av Tel (Bell) Forest 676

Bulgaria—P M Matheen, Comm-Gen, Bulgarian Section Dept Varied Industries, World's Fair Grounds

Canada—William Hutchnson Comm-Gen, W A Purns, Secretary, The Planters Hotel Tel (Bell) Main 137

Ceylon—Hon Stanley Bois Comm-Gen The Ceylon Court, World's Fair Grounds, or 5148 Washington Av Tel (Bell) Forest 1477 Russell Stanhope Asst Comm, 4471 Laclede Av

— 163 —

China—Prince Pu Lun Imperial Comm -Gen , Wong Kai-Kah, Imperial Vice-Comm 1385 Goodfellow Av , D Percebois Sec'y 5245 McPherson Av

Colombia—Di Santiago Cortez Chairman Ministry of Foreign Affairs, Bogota. Colombia

Costa Rica—Manuel Gonzales, Comm Gen , Harrison R Williams, Sec'y, 4024 Bell Av

Cuba—Esteban Duque Estrada Comm -Gen Antonio Carillo, Sec'y, 5745 Baltmer Av

Denmark—William Arup, Comm -Gen , Sutter and Joseph Avs , Hillside, Mo

Egypt—Herman Lawford Comm -Gen , The Westmoreland Hotel Tel (Bell) Lindell 2845

France—Michael Lagrave Comm -Gen , Felix Lamy, Secretary, Marcel Estieu, Attache, 3624 Lindell Boulevard Tel (Bell) Lindell 1674

Germany—Theodor Lewald Privy Councillor Imperial Comm -Gen , H Albert Asst Comm Otto Zippel Imperial Councillor Treasurer, 4936 Lindell Av Tel (Bell) Forest 1417

Great Britain—Col C M Watson R E , C B C M G Comm -Gen , Lucien Serrallier Secretary, The British Pavilion World's Fair Grounds Tel (Bell) 51

Guadaloupe—The President, Chairman, St Croix de la Ranclere Secretary, Point-a-Pitre Guadaloupe W I

Guatemala—Carlos F Irigoyen, Special Comm 3711 Olive St

Haytl—Edward Roumain Comm -Gen , Planters Hotel

Honduras—Salvador Cordova Comm -Gen , Agriculture Bldg World s Fair Grounds

British Honduras—Dr C Malhado Chairman, Belize British Honduras

Hungary—George De Szogyeny L I D , Comm -Gen , Westmoreland Hotel Tel (Bell) Lindell 2545

India—R Blechynden, Special Comm India Tea Assn , Southern Hotel Tel (Bell) Main 323-

Italy—Giovanni Bianchi, Comm -Gen , A. Alfant Secretary, Italian Pavilion, World s Fair Grounds

Japan—Baron Masanao Matsudaira Vice-Pres , Hajime Ota. Acting Comm -Gen , Japanese Pavilion, World s Fair Grounds, or Hamilton Hotel Tel (Bell) Forest 1205

Mexico—Eng Albino R Nuncio Comm -Gen Maximiliano M Chabert Secretary, Mexican Pavilion, World s Fair Grounds Tel (Kinloch) World s Fair Grounds Station 43

Morocco—James W Langermann Comm -Gen , Lorraine Hotel

Netherlands—Gerrit H Ter Brock Comm -Gen 1103 Jackson Place Tel (Bell) Main 2329

New Zealand—T E Donne Representative Hamilton Hotel

Nicaragua—Dr Leopoldo Ramirez Mairena, Pres , Alexander Bermudez Active Comm , Dr Rosendo Rubi Secretary, 3833 Pine St

Norway Frederick L M Wange Vice-Consul to St Louis St Louis Mo

Paraguay—Nicolas Angulo, Chairman, Ministry of Foreign Affairs Asuncion Paraguay

Peru—Alejandro Carland Comm -Gen , Peruvian Legation Washington

Persia—Lukian Khan Kelekian, Comm -Gen H S Tavshanjian, Com , Washington Hotel

Portugal—B C Cincinnato da Costa, Comm -Gen , Carlos A M Ribeiro Leirao Secretary The Washington Hotel Tel (Bell) Forest 1160

San Salvador—L Mejia Comm , Julio C Lecaros Asst Comm , Planters Hotel Tel (Bell) Main 437

San Domingo—Fidelio Despradel, Comm , Senor Galvan Comm , San Domingo City

Siam—James H Gore Comm -Gen , Nai Chuen Asst , 4184 Laclede Av

Spain—Mr Benlliure, Comm , Fine Arts Exhibit, Madrid Spain

Sweden—Col J A Ockerson Resident Comm , Axel Welin, Asst Comm. and Secretary, Swedish Pavilion, World s Fair Grounds

Turkey—Ch klb Bey (Minister to Washington) Comm -Gen Washington D C

Venezuela—Jesus Lameda, Comm -Gen , Eugenio M Aubard Secretary, 3808 Delmar Blvd

STATES, TERRITORIES AND POSSESSIONS

Alabama- Committee on Birmingham District Exhibit Fred M Jackson, Pres , J P Gibson Sec , J A MacKnight Special Rep , Rufus N Rhodes Culpepper Exum F W Dixon George H Clark

RHODE ISLAND BUILDING.

SOUTH DAKOTA BUILDING.

Alaska - Hon. Thomas Ryan, First Asst Sec of the Interior, Chairman, Gov John G Brady, Exec Comm. Honorary Commissioners M E Martin, Peter Jensen, O H Odsit, Frank Bach, Anthony Tubbs, L S Keller, D B . Mills, John Rustgard, John Goodell

Arizona—A J Doran, Chairman, B F Packard, Treas , H B St Claire, Sec , R N Leatherwood, Supt of Exhibits

Arkansas—George R Belding, Pres , J C Rembert Sec , Thomas W. Milan Mgr , George T Lake, John P Logan, A H Purdue, H T Bradford, Miss Lizzie Gage. Asst Lady Mgr , Charles Watkins.

California—Frank Wiggins, J A Filcher, E D Willis, Sec

Colorado—Gov James H Peabody Pres , T J O'Donnell Vice-Pres , Paul Wilson, Comm of Exhibits, I N Stevens, Sec , Mrs Lionel Rose Anthony Thomas F Walsh William S Sperry Harry Cassidy James A Wayne Asst to Comm -in-Chief

Connecticut—Frank L Wilcox, Pres Charles Phelps, V -Pres J H Vaill Sec and Treas , Edgar J Doolittle, Isaac W Birdseye, Gen Phelps Montgomery Mrs Louis R Cheney, Miss Anna Chappell, Mrs George M Knight

Georgia—Col Dudley Hughes Comm -Gen , Hugh V Washington Vice-Comm -Gen , Glasscock Barrett, Asst Comm -Gen , O B Stevens, Sec and Treas , W S Yates, Exec Comm

Hawaii—F W Macfarlane, Comm in Charge, W G Irwin Chm , C M Cooke V-Chm , J G Spencer, Sec , W O Smith Treas , Henry E Cooper, F J Amweg, F W Beardslee F A Schaefer, A L Louisson, Allen Herbert, W M Giffard H A Isenberg A Gartley J Kalamanaole, A N Kepoikai W W Dimond, J P Cooke, W W Harris, D D Baldwin J D Paris, J T Mon, E A Mott-Smith B F Dillingham, D Kalaouklani

Idaho—Gov J T Morrison, James E Steele Pres R W McBride. V -Pres , Mrs H W Mansfield, Sec , Martin J Wessels, Dr Harold J Read Clarence B Hurtt, Exec Committee

Illinois—H M Dunlap Pres , C N Travous, V -Pres , J P Mahoney 2d V -Pres John J Brown Sec , Walter Warder. Treas , Fred M Blount C F Coleman C C Craig Albert Campbell, James H Farrell D M Funk John H Miller John H Pierce W L Mounts, J N C Shumway, Thomas K Condit

Indiana—Newton W Gilbert. Chm James W Cockrum Sec , Henry W Marshall, W W Wicks W W Stevens W H O Brien Crawford Fairbanks D W Kinsey, N A Gladding, Frank C Ball, C C Shirley, Fremont Goodwine Joseph B Glass Stephen B Fleming, Melville W Mix, A C Alexander Asst Sec

Indian Territory--Hon Thomas Ryan, First Asst Sec of the Interior, Chairman Washington D C , F C Hubbard Exec Comm , Honorary Commissioners H B Johnson A J Brown, W L McWilliams, J E Campbell H B Spaulding, J J McAlester Wm Busby

Iowa—Commissioner at Large William Larrabee, Pres W W Witmer, District Commissioners Leroy A Palmer George M Curtis W F Harriman A -Pres , Thos Updegraff James H Trewin Samuel S Carruthers, S M Leach Treas S Bailey M D W T Shepherd C J A Ericson W C Whiting F R Conaway Sec

Kansas—John C Carpenter Pres J C Morrow V -Pres , R T Simons Treas , C H Luling Sec , William P Waggener

Kentucky—Gov J C W Feckham A Y Ford Chm , R E Hughes Sec , Charles G Spaulding V -Pres W H Cox Sam P Jones, W T Ellis, M H Crump Charles F Hoge J B Bowles A G Caruth, B L D Gufty, Garrett S Wall W J Worthington, Clarence Dallam W H Newman, Samuel Grabfelder

Louisiana—Gov William Wright Heard, Pres , J G Lee Sec Dr W C Stubbs State Comm , Chas Fuqua Asst Sec , Robert Glenk, Asst to State Comm , Col Charles Schuler. Judge Emil Kost H L Guevdan

Maine—Louis B Goodall Chm , Frank H Briggs Charles C Burrill, Lemuel Lane Henry W Sargent, Edward C Swett, Sec

Maryland—Gen L Victor Baughman Chm , Frederick P Stieff Treas , Francis E Waters Frank N Hoen, John E Hurst, William A Marburg Martin Wagner William H Graflin Wesley M Oler Thomas H Robinson, Jacob M Pearce Orlando Harrison Samuel K Dennis Sec

Massachusetts--Dr George Harris Pres , Mrs Sarah C Sears V -Pres , Mrs May Alden Ward Rec Sec , Wilson H Fairbank, Thomas B Fitzpatrick James M Perkins, Sec

Michigan--Gov Aaron T Bliss (ex-officio) Frederick B Smith, Pres , Austin Farrell, V-Pres , Roy S Barnhart Treas , Dr Aaron R Ingram Charles P Downey, Hal H Smith Sec , William A Hurst, Asst Sec

Minnesota--Conde Hamlin, Pres , J M Underwood V Pres Theodore L Hays Sec , C S Mitchell Gen Supt

Mississippi—Gov A H Longino (ex-officio) R H Henry Dr O B Quinn Chm, Frank Burkitt Sec, J H Enochs V P Still

Missouri—M T Davis Pres, Frank J Moss V-Pres, B H Bonfoy, Sec, W H Marshall Treas, N H Gentry, David P Stroup J O Allison J H Hawthorne, L F Parker

Montana—Lee Mantle Pres, Martin Maginnis V-Pres, C W Hoffman Treas, Paul McCormick Sec, W G Conrad H L Frank F A Heinze William Scallon Conrad Kohrs D R Peeler C J McNamara T L Greenough B F White, D McDonald J H Rice, W C Buskett Exec Comm

Nebraska—G W Waters, Pres, Peter Jinsen, V-Pres, Matt Miller Treas, H G Shedd Sec

Nevada—Gov John Sparks Pres, J A Yerington V-Pres and Exec Comm, C H E Hardin Sec

New Hampshire—Gen Chas S Collins Pres, Arthur C Jackson V-Pres and Exec Comm, Omar A Towne, Augustine R Myers, M McShan J Adam Graf, Orton B Brown

New Jersey—Foster M Voorhees Chief Comm, Elbert Rippleye, Edgar B Ward C L Breckenridge, Edward R Weiss J T McMurray Ira W Wood, W H Wiley Johnston Cornish Harry Humphries, R W Herbert Lewis T Bryant Sec

New Mexico—Charles A Spiess Pres, Carl A Dalles V-Pres, Arthur Seligman Treas W B Walton Sec, Eusebio Chacon F A Jones Herbert J Hagerman M W Porterfield, Gen Mgr

New York—Edward H Harriman Pres William Berri V-Pres Louis Stern, Chm of Exec Com, Edward Lauman Bill Treas Lewis Nixon Frank S McGraw, Mrs Norman L Mack Frederick R Green John C Woodbury John K Stewart James H Callanan John Young, Chas A Ball, Sec and Chief Exec Officer Mrs Dora Lyon Asst Sec

North Carolina—H H Brimley Comm-Gen

North Dakota—Gov Frank White Pres, Lieut-Gov David Bartlett Exec Comm R J Turner Sec H L Holmes Warren N Steel

Ohio—William F Burdell Pres L E Holden V-Pres Stacey B Rankin Exec Comm Edward Hagenbuch, Newell K Kennon David Friedman M K Gantz David H Moore

Oklahoma—Joseph Merbergen Chm Edgar E Marchant Sec, Otto A Shuttee Treas

Oregon—Jefferson Myers Pres W E Thomas V-Pres I S National Bank Treas Elmond C Giltner Sec F A Spencer Dave Rafferty J C Flinders, G P Hairy J H Albert Richard Scott Frank Williams F G Young C R Wide, W H Wehrung Gen Supt

Pennsylvania—Gov Samuel W Pennypacker Pres Frank G Harris Treas James H Lambert, Exec Officer, Bromley Wharton Sec William M Brown E B Hardenbergh Isaac B Brown John M Scott Henry F Watlon John C Grady William C Sproul William P Snyder J Henry Cochran Cyrus E Woods Theodore B Stulb John Hamilton William B Kirker William Wayne John A P Hoy Fred T Ikeler William H Ulrich A F Cooper, Frank B McClain George J Hartman William S Huyer Morris L Clothier Joseph M Gazzam George H Earle Jr Charles B Penrose George T Oliver H H Gilkyson Hiram Young Jas Pollock Jas McBrier

Philippine Islands—Dr W P Wilson Chm J L Irwin, Chief Clerk, Dr Gustave Niederlein Pedro A Paterno Leon Guerio Sec

Porto Rico—Jaime Annexy, Pres, Xavier Mariani, Gustavo Preston L A Castro

Rhode Island—Robert B Treat, Pres, William C Gleason V-Pres, Edwin G Pennimon Treas, George E Bill Sec Col Patrick E Hayes, Frank L Budlong George L Shepley George N Kingsbury Exec Comm

South Carolina—R Goodwin Rhett Chm Exec Comm Louis Appelt M R McSweeny Robert Aldrich R T Haynes J M Sullivan T C Duncan T J Moore Le Roy Springs R A Love Thomas Wilson R F Hamer Jr Altamont Moses E B Clark

South Dakota—S W Russell Pres L T Boucher, V-Pres, W D Saunders, Treas, George R Farmer, Sec

Tennessee—Gov James B Frazier Chm E C Lewis Ben F Dulaney Andrew M Soule E Watkins John I McNutt J M Shoftner John W Fry, Hu C Anderson, Thomas W Neal G L Raine Mrs J P Smutt Mrs Mary C Dorris Mrs A S Buchanan B A Enloe, Sec and Direc of Exhibits, D F Wallace, Jr, Asst Sec

Texas—John H Kirby Pres, L J Polk W W Seley Walter Tips, V-Prests, Royal A Ferris, Treas, Louis J Wortham Sec and Mgr Gov Joseph D Sayres Comm at large C H Allyn A H Belo Vories P Brown A P Bush Jr Edwin Chamberlain W C Connor H W Cortes C A Davies W W Dies T J Freeman Barnett Gibbs Clint Giddings Jr

J. N. Gilbert, Jack Gordon, A. T. Groom, B. F. Hammett, J. P. Harrison, L. J. Hart, H. E. Henderson, H. P. Hilliard, J. E. Hogg, F. P. Holland, A. W. Houston, E. L. Huffman, L. L. Jester, S. J. T. Johnston, R. M. Johnston, J. A. Kemp, E. J. Kleber, Otto Koehler, Harry Landa, N. H. Lassiter, R. R. Lockett, T. B. Love, A. L. Lowery, Geo. P. Brown, T. S. Miller, M. J. Moore, H. A. Morse, F. C. Jones, H. D. McDonald, H. F. MacGregor, H. A. O'Neal, E. B. Paddock, E. B. Perkins, Dr. T. A. Pope, Herbert Post, Dr. C. B. Raines, C. P. Russell, Sam Sanger, R. H. Sexton, Jesse Shain, W. B. Slosson, M. A. Spoonts, Paul Waples, George E. Webb, Nat M. Washer, George A. Wright, J. F. Davis, Wesley Love, S. H. Dixon, J. D. Lynch, Paul Jones, E. J. Fry, Sam Park, S. W. Blount, E. A. Blount, Fred W. Malley, F. C. Highsmith, R. T. Milner, John Durst, E. P. Styles, J. T. Richards, J. A. Farramore, P. G. R. Bell, James Langford, J. S. Kerr.

Utah—Gov. Heber M. Wells, Chm.; John Q. Cannon, Sec.; Hoyt Sherman, Samuel Newhouse, L. W. Shurtlyff, Willis Johnson, S. T. Whitaker, Director General.

Vermont—Gov. John G. McCullough, ex-officio Chm.; W. Seward Webb, Pres.; Arthur C. Jackson, 2d V.-Pres. and Exec. Comm.; Frederick G. Fleetwood, 3d V.-Pres.; Miss Mary Evarts, Sec.; J. C. Enright, Clerk and Counsel; F. W. Stanyan, Treas.

Virginia—C. W. Koiner, Pres.; G. E. Murrell, Sec.; W. W. Baker, Asst.; A. M. Bowman, J. L. Patton, O. W. Stone, B. C. Banks, J. Lyman Babcock.

Washington—A. L. Black, Pres.; Elmer E. Johnston, Exec. Comm.; W. W. Robertson, Edward C. Cheasty, Thomas Harrington, E. M. Hay, George Lindsley, G. W. R. Peaslee, Sec.; R. P. Thomas, W. W. Tolman.

West Virginia—N. E. Whitaker, Chm.; Fred Paul Grosscup, V.-Chm.; D. E. Abbott, Treas.; A. H. Winchester, Sec.; Frank Cox, E. C. Gerwig, John T. McCraw, R. M. Archer, Asst. Sec.

Wisconsin—W. D. Hoard, Pres.; A. J. Lindemann, V.-Pres.; Grant Thomas, Sec.; W. H. Flett, William A. Scott, Mrs. Lucy Morris, Mrs. Theodora Youmans.

Wyoming—Bryant B. Brooks, Pres.; George E. Pexton, V.-Pres.; Clarence B. Richardson, Comm.-in-Chief; William C. Deming, Sec.; Willis George Emerson, W. H. Holliday, J. L. Baird.

WEST VIRGINIA BUILDING.

ORIGIN AND HISTORY OF THE EXPOSITION.

The popular demand for a celebration of the centennial was first put in working order by a meeting of the Missouri Historical Society in September, 1898 which appointed a committee of 50 citizens to consider the various commemorative programs suggested in the press This committee finally recommended a submission of the question to a convention of delegates representing all the Louisiana Purchase States At the request of the committee, Governor Stephens of Missouri issued, December 13, 1898, a call inviting the Governors of the Louisiana Purchase States and Territories to appoint delegates to meet in St Louis, January 10, 1899.

A convention was accordingly held at the Southern Hotel on the appointed date and it was decided to hold a World's Fair as the most fitting commemoration of the 100th anniversary of the acquisition of the Louisiana territory An executive committee, with Hon D R Francis as chairman, was appointed to carry out the project, and this committee in turn selected a committee of 50 citizens of St Louis to raise the money necessary for the Fair Later the committee was increased to 200 It was decided that $15 000,000, the amount paid to France for the territory would be needed June 4 1900, Congress passed a bill promising Government support and an appropriation of $5 000 000 if the citizens of St Louis raised $10 000,000 The popular subscription of $5,000 000 from the citizens of St Louis was completed January 12, 1901, and on January 30, 1901, the Municipal Assembly of St. Louis passed an ordinance authorizing the issuance of $5 000,000 in city bonds for the Fair The bill appropriating $5,000,000 was passed by the House of Representatives February 9, 1901, and by the United States Senate, March 3, 1901 This bill was signed by President McKinley immediately and on March 12 following, he appointed the National Commission of nine members On August 20 1901, President McKinley issued a proclamation inviting all the nations of the world to participate in the Fair Ground was broken by President Francis in the presence of a vast throng December 20 1901 A bill permitting the postponement of the Fair from 1903 to 1904 was passed by Congress and approved by President Roosevelt June 25, 1902

Dedication Day.—On April 30, 1903, the grounds and buildings were dedicated with impressive ceremonies Theodore Roosevelt, President of the United States, delivered the dedicatory address Former President Grover Cleveland Hon D R Francis, President of the Louisiana Purchase Exposition and other prominent men, spoke Governors of various States, many of them accompanied by their military staffs, and many men of national fame also took part in the ceremonies In February, 1904, Congress passed a bill authorizing a loan by the Government to the Exposition of $4,600,000, to be repaid out of the revenue of the Exposition, and this bill was approved by President Roosevelt February 18, 1904

Opening Day—The Universal Exposition was opened April 30, 1904, in the presence of a brilliant and distinguished assemblage, including a delegation of the Senate and House of Representatives, the National Commission the Board of Lady Managers representatives of foreign Governments, Governors of States and their staffs in uniform, State Commissioners, United States Government Board, Exposition officials and others The ceremonies were conducted at the Louisiana Monument, Plaza of St Louis, starting promptly at 10 a m

Prayer by Frank W. Gunsaulus, of Chicago, was followed by an address by President Francis. Treasurer Wm H Thompson, as chairman of the Committee on Grounds and Buildings, introduced Isaac S Taylor, Director of Works, who delivered a gold key to the buildings to President Francis and presented diplomas to his staff. Director of Exhibits F J V Skiff followed in an address, and presented commissions to his staff. The Mayor of St Louis, Hon Rolla Wells, the President of the National Commission, Hon Thomas H Carter, Senator Henry E Burnham, for the United States Senate, Hon James A Tawney, in behalf of the House of Representatives, Edward H Harriman, for the Domestic Exhibitors, A R Nuncio Mexican Commissioner, for the foreign exhibitors spoke appropriately. As the representative of the President, Hon Wm H Taft, Secretary of War, concluded the speaking in an eloquent address, whereupon the President of the United States in the White House at Washington pressed a key and flashed a signal to the Exposition that started the machinery, unfurled the flags and set the great Cascades in motion

The attendance on opening day was 187,793, a larger opening day assemblage than was present at any previous exposition

EVENT COMMEMORATED.

"The annexation of Louisiana,' says a distinguished American historian, "was an event so portentous as to defy measurement. It gave a new face to politics and ranked, in historical importance, next to the Declaration of Independence and the adoption of the Constitution."

It not only saved our young and feeble Union from imminent internal and external peril in 1803, but assured the evolution of the peaceful and prosperous "world power' we are so proud of to-day. It provided the broader and safer foundation needed for future harmonious growth, and placed the Pacific Coast within our grasp. It supplied the keystone for a continental structure, the great valley which is our present seat of empire, the Republic's political center of gravity, whose cohesive attraction countervails all disintegrating forces and gives enduring strength to the National Constitution. We have seen how its great river system held East and West and North and South together through the awful storms of 1861-5.

After a century's experience of its immeasurable benefits, the American people could not permit the centennial of the treaty of cession to pass without a grand National commemoration. A convention of the Louisiana Purchase States asked St Louis, as then chief city, to take the lead in creating a colossal World's Fair as the most fitting commemoration. With the cordial and generous support of National, State and foreign Governments, she has done her best to break all World's Fair records and the Louisiana Purchase Exposition is the result.

The conclusion of the treaty of April 30 1803, by the great Napoleon, then First Consul of the French Republic and Thomas Jefferson, the author of the Declaration of Independence, then third President of the United States, put an end forever to dangerous frictions which had been a source of unceasing anxiety to the administrations of Presidents Washington and John Adams. It also prevented forever an im-

— 170 —

pending resumption of the strife, continued for more than a century, between France and Great Britain for ascendency in North America. During the Revolution thousands of hardy and adventurous settlers established themselves in Kentucky, Tennessee and on the upper Ohio. As they increased in numbers, they made a brilliant record as "The Rear Guard of the Revolution," and under the lead of George Rogers Clark they took and held the British posts at Kaskaskia and Vincennes, thereby enabling the United Colonies to obtain the Mississippi as their western boundary, from the Lake of the Woods to latitude 31 degrees, when the treaty of peace was arranged in 1783.

After the Revolution the rapidly increasing population of Kentucky, Tennessee and the Ohio Valley found themselves continually harassed by the hostilities of Indian allies of the British from the North and Indian allies of the Spanish from the South. At the same time they were wholly dependent on Mississippi river navigation for access to markets, and Spain denied their succession to the rights of free navigation accorded to British subjects by the treaty of 1763.

UTAH BUILDING.

Thus the Spanish posts north of latitude 31, and the free navigation of the Mississippi became the paramount questions with the Ohio Valley people. They had fought all their own battles so far, were prone to do so still and their threat to settle these burning questions for themselves, and in their own way, taxed the restraining influence and resources of President Washington to the utmost during the slow progress of the negotiations which, by the treaty of San Lorenzo in 1795, secured to them the right of free deposit at New Orleans. In 1801 the Western people were again intensely excited by rumors that Spain had secretly ceded Louisiana and the Floridas to France, and that the real destination of the army of 40,000 men sent by the First Consul, ostensibly to suppress insurrection in San Domingo, was to take military possession of Louisiana and the Floridas. Resistance to Napoleon's taking possession was the only thought of Western people, and they made it known that they would not wait for authority or assistance from the East, but would begin the fight at the first landing place with all the rifles and Indian allies they could muster

To reach a peaceful termination of this critical situation was the first care of Mr Jefferson when he took office as President in 1801 In the midst of the excitement, the Spanish Intendent at New Orleans made the situation more tense by suspending the right of deposit, and before a rectification of that outrage was procured from Madrid, Congress had met and adopted a very war-like tone

No man can say what glorious dream of restoring to France all her former North American possessions and converting them into a populous and prosperous "New France" was in Napoleon's mind when he extorted the secret treaty of San Ildefonso in 1800 from Spain He had a wonderful genius for statesmanship as well as for war, but the fates were against him or his European policy constrained him to cede Louisiana to the United States to prevent England from seizing it in the impending war

The steps taken by the American authorities to promote this decision on his part will not be recounted here They were certainly effective He sought to avoid a collision with us, to cement anew the bonds of friendship between France and the United States, and at the same time to build up this Republic as a great sea-power and commercial rival to England So he declared, and the cession of Louisiana has indisputably fulfilled all his expressed intentions

FACTS ABOUT ST. LOUIS.

St Louis, the city in which the great Louisiana Purchase Exposition is being held, is situated in the State of Missouri, on the west bank of the Mississippi River It is not a part of any county, being an independent city It has a population of 750 000, and is one of the most substantial communities financially in the world

DeSoto, Marquette and LaSalle had all visited the upper Mississippi River long before the expedition headed by Pierre Laclede Liguest set out from New Orleans on the trip which resulted in the founding of the City of St Louis Laclede, as Liguest was known among his companions, left New Orleans with his band of frontiersmen on August 3, 1763, to establish an Indian trading post in the North, the French Governor-General of the territory of Louisiana having granted to the explorer s firm, Maxent, Laclede & Co, of New Orleans, exclusive control of the fur trade with the Missouri and other tribes of Indians as far north as the River St Peter.

Three months were taken up by the journey up the Mississippi and when Laclede found the graceful curve in the river where the Merchants and Eads bridges now stand he immediately declared that the point should be the site for the post

After he had returned to Fort Chartres, where the party had left • • its stores and goods, a severe winter set in and it was not until February 14, 1764, that Auguste Chouteau, then in his fourteenth year, arrived at the site in charge of an expedition of 30 men, which Laclede had placed at his command Under young Chouteau's direction the site for the future city was cleared

The first tool shed and log cabins built by the pioneers stood on what is now the block bounded by Broadway and Sixth St, Washington Av and St Charles St Laclede, who was a native of France, named the trading post St Louis, after the patron saint of the French sovereign Louis XV, although France had ceded the territory to Spain in the year 1762

Under the authority of the Spanish viceroy of Louisiana, Rios arrived on August 11 1768 to take possession of the colony The settlers were hostile to Spanish rule and that Government's occupation proved rather profitless

In 1800 Spain ceded the Province of Louisiana back to France, St Louis being part of the territory, but three years later, in 1803 the United States Government purchased Louisiana from Napoleon and from that date the city became a part of the great American Republic

At first the growth of St Louis was very slow In the year 1800, when 36 years of age, it contained less than 1,000 souls, and in 1822, although then 58 years in existence, its population was less than 5,000 Later on, when the place began to get its real growth, it moved forward with giant strides, and now ranks as the fourth city in the United States, New York, Chicago and Philadelphia alone leading it

During the early part of the century just closed, St Louis became the center of the vast steamboat trade which was built up on the Mississippi River and later on the Missouri When the bridges were built across the Mississippi River, connecting the city with the Illinois shore, river traffic began to wane, the railroads succeeding to the business The river interest however, is still a large one, and St Louis is still the center of the traffic

St Louis is the gateway for the trade of the entire Southwest, and in many lines of jobbing and manufacturing it leads every city in the country, and in some few outranks any city in the world It is centrally located, being midway between the North and South, and far enough West not to be classed as an Eastern city, while at the same time, it is far enough East not to be a distinctively Western city, now that the great territory between it and the Pacific slope has been well settled and built up

St Louis far exceeds any other district in the United States in the output of manufactured tobacco It also contains the largest tobacco factory in the world The biggest brewery in America is situated in St Louis, and the beers of this city are sold in all parts of the globe The largest shoe house in the world is to be found in St Louis, and the city is one of the biggest points on the globe for the manufacture and wholesaling of shoes In each of the lines of wholesale hardware, wholesale drugs and wholesale woodenware, the city possesses a concern which surpasses in volume of business any house in a similar line on earth St Louis is the greatest horse and mule market and a leading saddlery market of the world The biggest chemical manufacturing plant in America is situated here, and so is the country's greatest cracker factory The city also leads the country in the manufacture of white lead and jute bagging It has the largest brick works, the largest sewer pipe factory and the largest electric plant on the continent, and it manufactures more street cars than any city in the world, shipping them to all sections of the globe. In the jobbing of dry goods, millinery, hats and gloves, and groceries, St Louis ranks among the foremost on the continent

Historic Spots —A ride along Broadway, northward to the Chain of Rocks, and a walk of a mile further, brings us to the scene where

WASHINGTON BUILDING.

Lewis and Clark started on their great Northern exploration, which ended at Oregon on the Pacific

At Broadway and Walnut streets the cobble stones of civilization are the tombstones over the grave of the great Indian Chief, Pontiac, who waged merciless war against the British and who led the tribes in their attack at Braddock's defeat near Fort Du Quesne In the Southern Hotel, the visitor will view a modern structure which stands on the site of the stockade the headquarters, in 1769 of St Ange, the French colonial Governor of Louisiana at that period A tablet in the corridor of the hotel marks the burial place of Pontiac, Chief of the Illinois James Fenimore Cooper in his tales of the Prairie and the Pathfinder describes this great Indian nation

The old Government house, in which the **transfer of the upper Louisiana Territory** was made, March 10 1804, by Governor Delassus to Captain Amos Stoddard, representing the United States, stood on a site now marked by the southeast corner of Main and Walnut Sts

On Walnut St, between Second and Third Sts, the antiquarian will find a curious pile of architecture in the old French Catholic Cathedral, which was finished April 14, 1775

Probably the last slaves sold west of the Mississippi River were those who were offered at public auction from the grimy blocks on either side of the Court House, standing on Broadway between Chestnut and Market Sts, a description of which many visitors to the Exposition have read in Winston Churchill's "Crisis" a story of antebellum period in St Louis Thomas Benton the statesman, made one of his famous pro-slavery speeches from the same steps The Court House was commenced in 1839 and was completed in July, 1862

Monk s Mound, eight miles from East St Louis by the Collinsville electric trolley line, brings the student of the prehistoric race to face with the age of the **Mound Builders** This vast pyramid the largest of the relics left by an unknown people, whom even the Indians have forgotten takes its name from the Trappist Monks who at one time had a monastery on its summit The mound rises 100 feet above the surrounding plain It is surrounded by a series of smaller mounds, stretched in a semi-circle about the principal pile

A number of old French houses built in the seventeenth century are yet standing in Cahokia, Ill, reached by a ferry trip across the river from Carondelet and a drive eastward of four miles Cahokia is the oldest French village in the Mississippi Valley A church erected 160 years ago is now used as a schoolhouse

Florissant is a suburb of St Louis, reached by trolley line from the western part of the city It is another French settlement antedating the founding of St Louis by several years

Kaskaskia, a short distance by boat on the Mississippi was the **first capital of Illinois.** Now it is a small fishing village At one time it was the headquarters of the French provincial army Ruins of military posts may still be seen there

St Genevieve is a city from which the Mississippi moved away, leaving it miles from the stream It is the oldest town in Missouri, and at one time furnished all of the supplies of St Louis

General Fremont, the great Pathfinder of the Rockies lived in St Louis and started from the city on his remarkable exploration of the unknown West

St Louis was the outfitting point for most of the **gold hunters** who were attacked by the '49 fever and crossed the plains to California

The **Santa Fe trail** started from St Louis, which became the outfitting point for all exploration of the arid West and Southwest The pony express followed

The **United** States arsenal, erected by the Government in 1828, is to be seen at Second and Arsenal Sts It was used as a general supply depot for ordnance and quartermaster's stores

It was from **Jefferson Barracks**, just south of the city limits, that the famous old Third Cavalry, with General Robert E Lee as colonel, and General Albert Sidney Johnston and General Jubal Early as majors, with General Winfield Scott Hancock as a captain and General Fitz Hugh Lee as lieutenant, marched out for the war with Mexico. General Ulysses S Grant also departed for Mexico from this post. Only a few years later all but Grant and Hancock were famous Confederate soldiers Grant and Lee became the generalissimos of the opposing forces

The immortal General U S Grant hauled logs from his country home into St Louis, along the Gravois road, a street in the southern part of the city, still crooked and still bearing the same name. The house in which he was married to Miss Julia Dent is standing on the corner of Fourth and Cerre Sts. (The old Grant log cabin is shown at the World's Fair) Two blocks further west on the same street is the house in which General Winfield Scott Hancock was married. The residence of General William Tecumseh Sherman is shown on Garrison Av General Sherman and wife are buried in Calvary cemetery

At the intersection of Lindell and Channing Avs. with Olive St the visitor on the way to the Exposition will pass over the exact site of **Camp Jackson**, a Confederate stronghold which was captured by the Federal troops under Colonel Lyon, who marched there from the arsenal

---

Baseball Parks —National League, Vandeventer Av and Natural Bridge Rd , American League, Grand and Sullivan Avs

Block and House Numbers —St Louis has a system of numbering whereby it is very easy for strangers to learn how to reach any desired point Streets running east and west have the buildings on them numbered from the river, each succeeding block beginning with a new No 100, thus, 2d St begins the No 200, while 12th St. is 1200 west, and so on Streets running north and south are numbered from Market St as the dividing line as far west as 28th St , where it merges into Laclede Av , and from there west the latter street is the dividing line Each block north of Market St is numbered an additional hundred north and each block south of that thoroughfare an additional hundred south Thus, Franklin Av , which is nine blocks north of Market St , is No 900 north and Chouteau Av , which is ten blocks south of Market St , is No 1000 south All houses on the north side of the streets running east and west are given odd numbers, while buildings on the south side have the even numbers On the streets running north and south the odd numbers are on the west side of the street and the even numbers on the east side

Public Buildings.—Among the public buildings in St Louis are the U. S Custom House, occupying the block from 8th to 9th and Olive to Locust Sts the Court House, which takes up the block from 4th to Broadway and from Chestnut to Market Sts , the City Hall, occupying an area extending from Market St to Clark Av. and from 12th to 13th Sts , the Four Courts, Jail and Morgue, bounded by Clark Av ,

Spruce, 11th and 12th Sts., the Board of Education building at 9th and Locust

Office Buildings.—Among the prominent buildings of the city are Boatmen's Bank, 4th and Washington Av., St. Louis Union Trust, 4th and Locust Sts., Security, 4th and Locust Sts., Rialto, Olive and 4th Sts., Laclede, Olive and 4th Sts. Mississippi Valley Trust, 4th and Pine Sts., Granite, 4th and Market Sts., Gay, 3d and Pine Sts., Roe, Broadway and Pine St., Houser, Broadway and Chestnut St., National Bank of Commerce, Broadway and Olive St., Commonwealth Trust, Broadway and Olive St., Wells, Broadway and Olive St., Mechanics National Bank, Broadway and Locust St.; Mermod & Jaccard, Broadway and Locust St., Equitable 6th and Locust Sts., Oriel, 6th and Locust Sts., Carleton, 6th and Olive Sts., Commercial 6th and Olive Sts., Missouri Pacific, 7th and Market Sts., Lincoln Trust, 7th and Chestnut Sts. Wainwright, 7th and Chestnut Sts., Columbia, 8th and Locust Sts., Holland, 7th bet Pine and Olive Sts., Missouri Trust, 7th and Olive Sts., Chemical, 8th and Olive Sts., Mercantile Trust, 8th and Locust Sts.; Century 9th, Olive to Locust Sts.; Frisco, 9th and Olive Sts., Odd Fellows, 9th and Olive Sts., Burlington, Olive bet 8th and 9th Sts., Benoist, 9th and Pine Sts., Star, 12th and Olive Sts., Studio, Jefferson and Washington Avs., Y M C A, Grand and Franklin Avs. Masonic Hall and Odeon, Grand her Bell and Finney Avs.

Business District.—The principal business district of the city lies between Franklin Av. on the north Market St. on the south and east of 12th St. Washington Av. is one of the best-built wholesale thoroughfares in the world. Broadway, which has a total length of over 15 miles under that official name, and which extends about 22 miles all told, including streets which are virtual continuations of it, is a leading north and south retail street. Olive St. is a prominent east and west avenue for retail trade

Cupples Station—Most of the large wholesale grocery and many of the other jobbing lines are located in what is known as the Cupples Station, which is situated from 7th to 9th Sts and from Clark Av to Poplar St. Railroad switches enter these series of warehouses, which are alongside of the Terminal Association tracks. In this way the concerns occupying the buildings do their loading and unloading direct to and from the trains thereby avoiding drayage and hauling charges and delays. The Cupples Station is unique in that no other city in the world possesses anything similar to it

Cab Rates—With one horse 1 person, 1 mile, 25c, 2d m, 1 or 2 persons, 25c each, ¼ mile additional, 1 or 2 persons, 15c, 1 stop, 10 min free additional stops of 10 min, 10c, small packages inside, free, carried outside, 10c. Per hour, within 3 m of Court House, 1 or 2 persons, 75c, each additional ¼ hr, 20c, beyond 3 m limit, 1st hour, $1.00, each additional ¼ hr, 25c. While waiting, per hr, 75c. With two horses 1 person, 1 m, 50c, each additional m, 1 or 2 persons, 50c, per hr, 1 or 2 persons, $1.50, each additional hr, $1.00, double fare from midnight to 6 a m

The ordinance requires that rates must be kept posted in the vehicle. Passengers must notify driver when starting that they desire to use the vehicle by the hour otherwise the driver may assume that he is hired by the mile. Strangers giving checks for baggage to drivers should note number of conveyance or the figure on the badge worn by the driver, and make an arrangement as to the fare in order to avoid misunderstanding. In case of trouble of any kind with the hackman, make prompt complaint to the nearest policeman

Cemeteries.—Bellefontaine and Calvary cemeteries are beautiful stretches of rolling landscape contiguous to one another, in the north end of the city, and embracing nearly 700 acres.

Clubs.—St. Louis, Lindell Bl., west of Grand Av.; University, Grand Av. and Washington Bl.; Columbian, Lindell Bl. and Vandeventer Av.; Concordia, Lindell Bl., west of Grand Av.; Union, Lafayette and Jefferson Avs.; Mercantile, 7th and Locust Sts.; Missouri Athletic, 4th and Locust Sts.; Elks, Holland Bldg.; St. Louis Woman's Club, Washington Av., near Grand Av. Besides the city clubs there are the following country clubs: St. Louis Country, Clayton Rd., opposite the town of Clayton; Log Cabin, Clayton Rd., beyond the St. Louis Country; Field, north of city on Burlington R. R.; Kinloch, Scudder Av. and Suburban Ry.; Florissant Valley, Natural Bridge Rd. and Suburban and Wabash tracks; Glen Echo, on opposite side of

WISCONSIN BUILDING.

Wabash tracks from Florissant Valley; Normandy, St. Charles Rock Rd. beyond Wabash tracks.

Political Clubs.—Jefferson Club (Democratic), Grand Av. and West Pine Bl.; St. Louis Hamilton Club (Republican), 2721 Pine St.; Good Government Club (Republican), 2300 Eugenia St.

Commercial Organizations—Among the commercial exchanges and business organizations of St. Louis are the Merchants' Exchange, 3d St. from Pine to Chestnut; Stock Exchange, 314 N. 4th St.; Cotton Exchange, Main and Walnut Sts.; Live Stock Exchange, National Stock Yards, East St. Louis, Ill.; Real Estate Exchange, 110 N. 8th St.; Lumberman's Exchange, 319 N. 4th St.; Builders' Exchange, 202 N. 9th St.; Mining Stock Exchange, 411 Olive St.; Furniture Board of Trade, 110 N. 8th St.; Business Men's League, ground floor Mercantile Club, 7th and Locust Sts.; Interstate Merchants' Association, Centuty Bldg, 9th and Olive Sts Bureau of Information of Associations, for visiting merchants, their families and friends, at 1824 Olive St., Manutacturers Association 2d and Pine Sts, Latin-American Club and Foreign Trade Association, 110 N 4th St

Express Companies and Charges—Adams 407 N 4th American-European, 407 N 4th, American, 417 N 4th, National, 708 Washington Av Northern Pacific, 708 Washington Av, Pacific, 412-414 N 4th, Southern, 407 N 4th, United States 121 N 4th Wells, Fargo & Co 709 Olive All these companies except the Pacific, have a joint office on the World's Fair Grounds in the Model City (See "Classified Information") The Pacific has an office in the Wabash station opposite the entrance at De Baliviere Av and Forsythe junction All companies will have a free delivery inside the grounds No charge is made by express companies for delivering packages in the district of the city bounded by the river on the east St Louis Av on the north No 2400 on the south, and Grand Av on the west, except between Laclede and Page Avs, where the western limit extends as far as Vandeventer Av Outside of this district and the World's Fair Grounds, a charge is made of 15 cents for packages weighing less than 10 lbs 25 cents for packages from 10 to 25 lbs 50 cents for packages from 25 to 50 lbs and when above the latter weight the charges are based on the weight and distance

Foreign Consuls in St. Louis.—Argentine Republic, Gus V Brecht, 1201 Cass Av Austrian-Hungarian Ferdinand Diehm, Olive southeast corner 4th St Belgium, Louis Seguenot 119 N 7th St, Brazil Alphonso De Figueiredo 400 S Broadway, Colombia, James Arbuckle 110 N 7th St, Costa Rica, Eben Richards 420 Olive St, Danish, C E Ramlose, Broadway, northwest corner Hickory St, France, Louis Seguenot, 119 N 7th St German Empire, Dr Friedrich C Rieloff, 214 N 4th St, Great Britain, Western Bascome, 313 N 9th St, Greece, Demetrius Jannopoulo 100 N 2d St Guatemala, Nicaragua and Honduras, L D Kingsland 1521 N 11th St, Holland B B Haagsma 211 N 7th St Italy, Domencio Ginocchio 713 N 3d St Liberia, Hutchins Inge, 1107 Clark Av Mexico Ratel P Serrano 421 Olive St, Netherlands B B Haagsma 211 N 7th St, Persia Milton C Scropvan, 3556 Olive St Spain Jose M Trigo 212 Pine St, Switzerland, Jacob Buff 214 N 4th St

Handsome Homes—It is in its residence district that St Louis stands pre-eminent No city in the world has so many palatial homes grouped together Extending along the north side of the east end of Forest Park and directly facing it from Kingshighway to Union Bl are stretched along Lindell Av, or Forest Park Terrace as it is officially known a group of most magnificent mansions Westmoreland Place, just one block further north, and Portland Place the next street north of Westmoreland are built up with the same character of palatial homes Kingsbury Place and Washington Terrace, just to the west and north of the districts named, contain residences of the same spacious and costly style Vandeventer Place which extends from Grand to Vandeventer Av just north of Morgan St is a somewhat older district which is also noted for its handsome homes Lindell Bl West Pine Bl Washington Bl, Berlin Av Hortense Place, Cabanne Place and various other West End streets also contain many handsome residences On the south side of the city the handsomest homes are located in what is known as the Compton Heights section, a most attractive and picturesque locality

Hotels in Business District.—Jefferson, 12th and Locust Sts., Planters', 4th and Pine Sts., Southern, Broadway and Walnut St., St. Nicholas, 8th and Locust Sts., Lindell, Washington Av and 6th St.; Laclede, Chestnut and 6th Sts., Terminal, in Union Station, Madison, Broadway and Chestnut St., Moser, 809 to 813 Pine St., Rozier, 13th and Olive Sts.; Merchants, 12th and Olive Sts., St. James, Broadway and Walnut St.; Barnum, 6th St and Washington Av., Hurst's, 6th St and Lucas Av., Benton (bachelor), 819 Pine St., Pontiac, 19th and Market Sts., Metropolitan, 19th and Market Sts., Portland, 1817 Market St., Milton, 18th and Chestnut Sts., Horn's, 7th and Pine Sts., Stratford, 8th and Pine Sts., Hotel de Paris, 209½ N 8th St., Charleville, 2227 Locust St., Garni, Jefferson Av and Olive St., Grand Central, Jefferson Av and Pine St. South Side, Broadway and Pestalozzi St.

Hotels in Residence District.—Washington, Kingshighway and Washington Bls., Buckingham Club Kingshighway and West Pine Bls., West End, Vandeventer Av and West Bell Pl., Pechmann, Olive St and Boyle Av., Rebman, Olive St and Boyle Av. Westmoreland, Maryland and Taylor Avs., Grand Avenue, Grand Av and Olive St., Beers, Grand Av. and Olive St. Hamilton, Hamilton and Maple Avs., Monticello, Kingshighway and West Pine Bls., Usona, Kingshighway and McPherson Av., Lorraine, Lindell Bl and Boyle Av., Berlin, Taylor and Berlin Avs., Beresford (and Annex), 4143 to 4149 Lindell Bl.; Franklin Sarah St and Westminster Pl., Normandie, Channing and Franklin Avs., Hilton, 1000 N Grand Av., Granville, 914 N Grand Av., Charlemont, Washington and Vandeventer Avs., Henrietta 4487 Washington Bl., Cordova, 4056 McPherson Av.; Norfolk, 4265 Olive St., West Belle, 4024 West Belle Pl., Clarkville Terrace, 3645 Olive St. Sherwood, 4323 Morgan St.; Hoffman, Locust St and Compton Av., Crescent, 28th and Locust Sts.; Hartford, 2912 Washington Av., Blue Grass Bachelor, 4040 Olive St., Bachelor, 2846 Olive St.

Hotels at Fair Grounds.—"Inside Inn," located inside the Exposition grounds, at southeast corner, near Clayton and Oakland Av. entrance; "Outside Inn," northwest corner Delmar Bl and Hamilton Av., Napoleon Bonaparte, De Baliviere Av., near entrance, American, De Baliviere Av adjoining entrance, Epworth, north of grounds at Washington and Melville Avs., Christian Endeavor adjoining World's Fair Grounds on the south, Grand View Fraternal, a short distance west of Christian Endeavor, Cottage City, containing 100 cottages, just outside of an enclosure on the Clayton Rd between Skinker Rd (University Bl) and Pennsylvania Av., Fraternal Home, Clayton Av., just east of Cottage City, Forest Park, Clayton Rd just east of Fraternal Home, Forest Park University, on south line of Forest Park, near southeast corner of grounds, West Park Cottage, near corner of Tamm and West Park Avs. 4 blocks south of grounds, Billon, Billon and West Park Avs., 3 blocks south of grounds; Kenilworth West Park and Billon Avs., Oakland, Clayton and Oakland Avs., at southeast corner of grounds, States, near southeast corner of grounds Iowa, Clayton and Billon Avs. 1 block from southeast corner of grounds, Wise Av Apartments south of grounds 3 blocks from Cheltenham Gate, Visitors' World's Fair, Kingsbury Bl and Clara Av., 4 blocks from De Baliviere Av (Lindell) entrance, Heights Hotel Cottages, near southwest corner of grounds, Walther, Delmar Bl and Adelaide Av., opposite Delmar Garden.

Camping Grounds.—(Board floors and water-proof tents are provided at these places) University Park Encampment, Pennsylvania Av, adjoining grounds on west, Woman's Magazine Encampment, University Heights, north of Delmar Bl, a few blocks from northwest corner of grounds, Oklahoma World's Fair Association, west of grounds, World's Fair Tenting Association, at Clayton Bl, 1 block west of grounds

Libraries.—Public, northwest corner 9th and Locust Sts, Mercantile, southwest corner Broadway and Locust St

Monuments—Some famous monuments of great people are to be found in St Louis, notably some heroic statues of Shakespeare, Humboldt and Columbus in Tower Grove Park, statues of Washington and Benton in Lafayette Park, statue of Grant in the City Hall Park, Frank P Blair, at the eastern entrance to Forest Park, and Bates, in the same park, bronze busts of the master composers, placed on marble shafts, encircling the music stand in Tower Grove Park the Schiller monument in St Louis Park, and several other isolated pieces of more or less interest. At a conspicuous point on the main driveway in Tower Grove Park the visitor will be interested in the Neilsen mulberry, which grew from a slip cut from the tree that shades Shakespeare's tomb at Stratford-on-the-Avon The spot where the slip is planted was marked by Adelaide Neilsen during a visit to St Louis

Museum of Arts—The St Louis Museum of Fine Arts is located at 19th and Locust Sts

Nearby Places—Both Meramec Highlands and Creve Coeur Lake are within 40 minutes' ride of the Exposition The route lies through exquisite bits of scenery One mile west of the Exposition site lies the little town of Clayton, the capital of St Louis county.

Among other attractive suburban places about St Louis are Kirkwood, Webster Groves, Normandy, Clayton, Piasa Bluffs, and many lovely country homes in St Louis county

Newspapers—Republic 7th and Olive Sts, Globe-Democrat, 6th and Pine Sts, Post-Dispatch, Broadway south of Olive St, Star, 12th and Olive Sts, Chronicle 6th St, south of Market St, World, Chestnut, west of 9th St, Westliche Post and Anzeiger, Broadway and Market St, Amerika, 3d, south of Chestnut

Parks—Forest Park contains 1,374 acres and is the second largest municipal park in America It claims the interest of the visitor to the Exposition in a distinctive degree, since the western half is occupied by the main spectacle of the World's Fair The eastern half has been left unspoiled of its natural beauty with miles of hard roadways, good in all weather The **Missouri Botanical Garden**, famous throughout the world as Shaw's Garden, contains 50 acres of the most superb botanical treasures in America. Near Shaw's Garden, and indeed a former part of the Shaw estate, is **Tower Grove Park,** in which some of the most resplendent examples of landscaping in the world may be enjoyed It also contains many fine statues. **Lafayette Park**, a smaller spot of beauty, reached by the Park Av cars, contains a statue of Washington, by Houdan, the French sculptor, whose conception of the first great American was taken from a mold of his illustrious subject It is pronounced to be one of the finest statues extant of the Father of His Country Carondelet Park, O'Fallon Park, Laclede Park, Carr Park, St Louis Park, Compton Hill Reservoir Park and Benton Park are other recreation grounds which possess their individual interest

Race Tracks—Fair Association, Grand Av and Natural Bridge Rd , Delmar, Delmar Bl west of city limits, Kinloch, Kinloch Park Station, St Louis County, on Wabash and Suburban roads, Union, Union Av and Natural Bridge Rd

River Bridges.—The Eads bridge at St Louis is the greatest bridge, over one of the greatest rivers in the world It was the conception of a great St Louis genius, Captain James B Eads, the first engineer to successfully demonstrate that millions of tons of steel and stone might rest safely on beds of shifting quicksand This monument to his genius made possible the marvelous Brooklyn Suspension bridge Both structures were built in caissons sunk through quicksand to a solid bedrock The total cost of the bridge, including approaches, was $10,000,000 The Merchants Bridge, farther up the river, is a fine example of the truss principle as applied to bridge building

Summer Gardens—(Where opera or vaudeville is given)—Delmar Garden, Delmar Bl, west of city limits, Suburban Park, Irving Av and N Market St Forest Park Highlands, Berthold and Sublette Avs , Koerner's Garden Kingshighway and Arsenal St , West End Heights, opposite southwest corner World's Fair Grounds, Uhrig s Cave, Washington and Jefferson Avs . Hashagen's Park, Grand Av and Meramec St Mannion Park, 8000 S Broadway Eclipse Park, Virginia Av and Primm St . Lemp s Park, 13th and Utah Sts

Theaters—Olympic Broadway and Walnut St , Century, 9th and Olive Sts Columbia 6th and St Charles Sts , Grand Opera House Market and 6th Sts Imperial, 10th and Pine Sts , Havlin's 6th and Walnut Sts , Crawford, 14th and Locust Sts , Standard, 7th and Walnut Sts ; Odeon Grand and Finney Avs , Grand Music Hall Olive and 13th Sts , Coliseum Locust and 13th Sts , Pickwick, Washington and Jefferson Avs

Union Station.—Most of the visitors to the Exposition will step from the trains into the Union Station the largest railway station in the world The architectural nobility of its great facade, stretching 606 feet along Market St from 18th to 20th Sts , is admitted to be the finest ever applied to this style of building It has a train shed 600 feet wide, by more than 700 feet long, covering more than 11 acres There are 32 tracks The station cost $7,000,000

Weather in St. Louis—The weather that visitors may expect is shown by the records of the United States Weather Bureau The "normals' of averages of the temperature at St Louis during the 33 years that the weather bureau has had a station in St Louis are as follows May, 66 1, June, 75 4 July, 79 4, August 77 6, September, 70 2, October 58 7, November, 44 3

The Louisiana Purchase Exposition is to last seven months, instead of six months, as did the Columbian and Paris Expositions Opening April 30, the Louisiana Purchase Exposition will not close until December 1 1904 The reason for this is that as a rule the weather at St Louis during October and November is peculiarly agreeable The night weather throughout the season during which the Exposition will be open is very pleasant

ST. LOUIS AND GUIDING SPIRITS.
At Base of Apotheosis of St. Louis (Main Plaza).

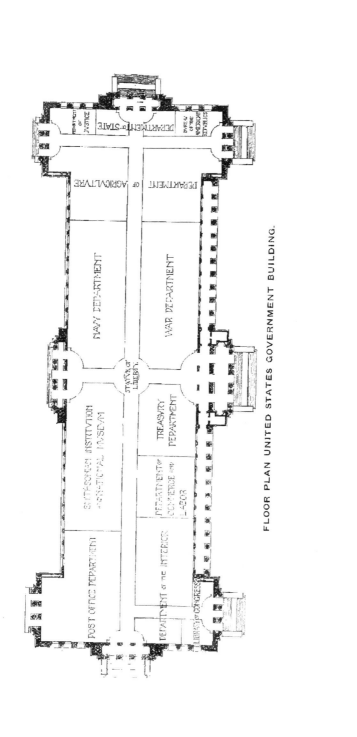

FLOOR PLAN UNITED STATES GOVERNMENT BUILDING.

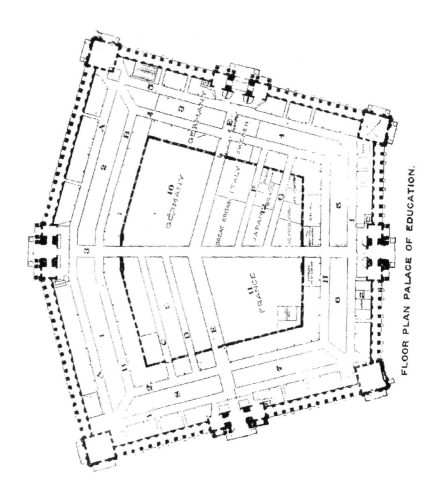

FLOOR PLAN PALACE OF EDUCATION.

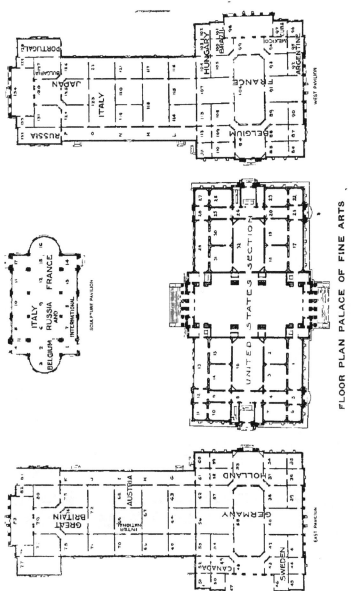

FLOOR PLAN PALACE OF FINE ARTS

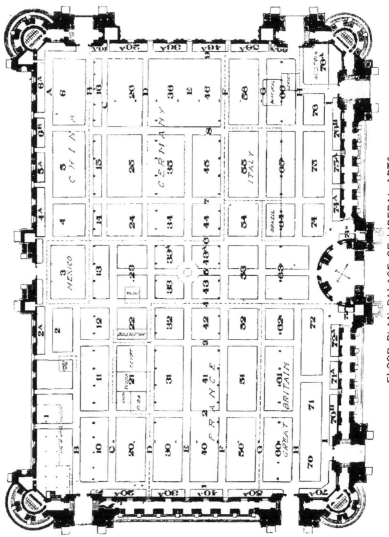

FLOOR PLAN PALACE OF LIBERAL ARTS.

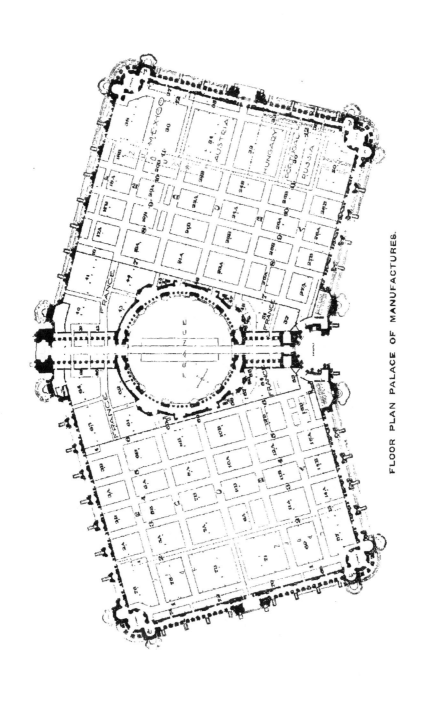

FLOOR PLAN PALACE OF MANUFACTURES.

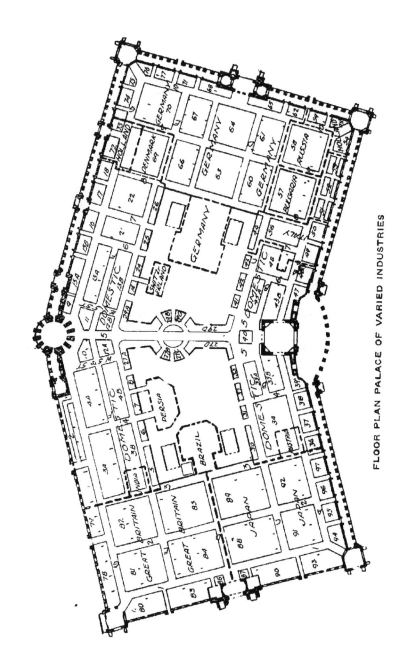

FLOOR PLAN PALACE OF VARIED INDUSTRIES

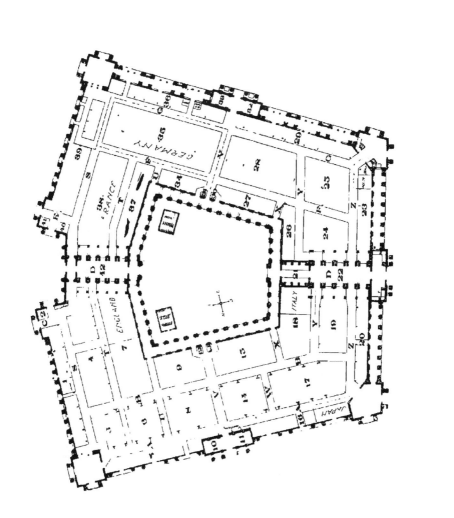

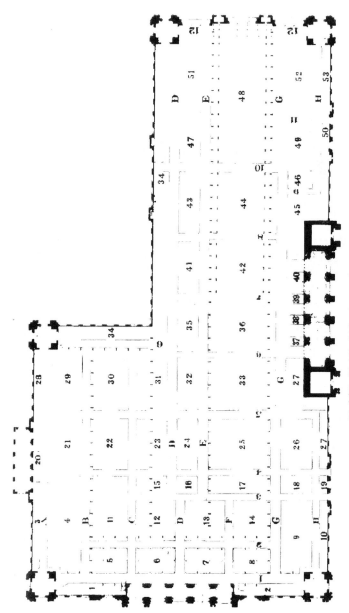

FLOOR PLAN PALACE OF MACHINERY.

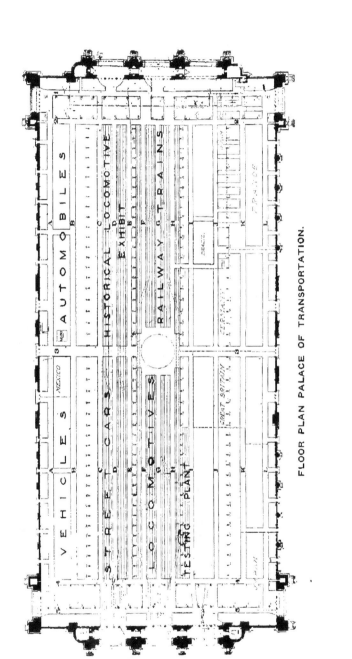

FLOOR PLAN PALACE OF TRANSPORTATION.

FLOOR PLAN PALACE OF MINES AND METALLURGY.

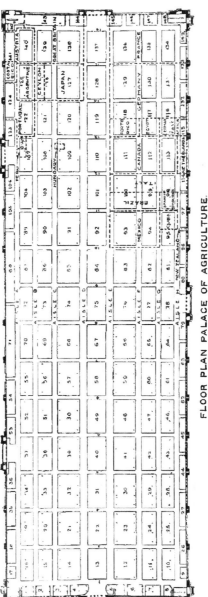

FLOOR PLAN PALACE OF AGRICULTURE.

— 197 —

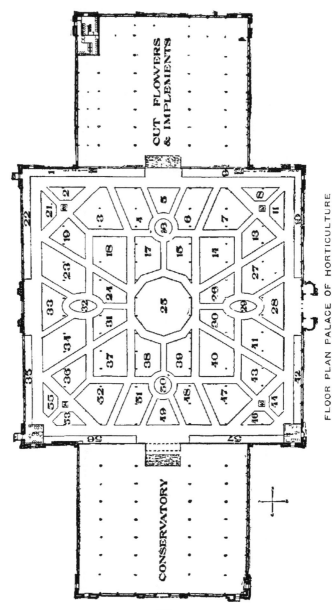

CUT FLOWERS & IMPLEMENTS

CONSERVATORY

FLOOR PLAN PALACE OF HORTICULTURE

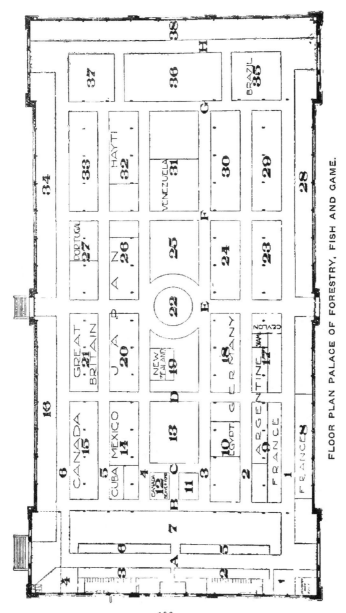

FLOOR PLAN PALACE OF FORESTRY, FISH AND GAME.

INDEX.

CPSIA information can be obtained
at www.ICGtesting.com
Printed in the USA
LVHW082236020222
710124LV00009B/382